# MznLnx

*Missing Links Exam Preps*

Exam Prep for

## Calculus Early Transcendentals

### Stewart, 4th Edition

The MznLnx Exam Prep is your link from the texbook and lecture to your exams.
The MznLnx Exam Preps are unauthorized and comprehensive reviews of your textbooks.

All material provided by MznLnx and Rico Publications (c) 2010
Textbook publishers and textbook authors do not particpate in or contribute to these reviews.

## MznLnx

Rico
Publications

*Exam Prep for Calculus Early Transcendentals*
4th Edition
Stewart

*Publisher:* Raymond Houge
*Assistant Editor:* Michael Rouger
*Text and Cover Designer:* Lisa Buckner
*Marketing Manager:* Sara Swagger
*Project Manager, Editorial Production:* Jerry Emerson
*Art Director:* Vernon Lowerui

*Product Manager:* Dave Mason
*Editorial Assitant:* Rachel Guzmanji
*Pedagogy:* Debra Long
*Cover Image:* Jim Reed/Getty Images
*Text and Cover Printer:* City Printing, Inc.
*Compositor:* Media Mix, Inc.

(c) 2010 Rico Publications
ALL RIGHTS RESERVED. No part of this work covered by the copyright may be reproduced or used in any form or by an means--graphic, electronic, or mechanical, including photocopying, recording, taping, Web distribution, information storage, and retrieval systems, or in any other manner--without the written permission of the publisher.

For more information about our products, contact us at:
Dave.Mason@RicoPublications.com

For permission to use material from this text or product, submit a request online to:
Dave.Mason@RicoPublications.com

Printed in the United States
ISBN:

# Contents

**CHAPTER 1**
*Functions and Models* — 1

**CHAPTER 2**
*Principles of Problem Solving* — 10

**CHAPTER 3**
*Differentiation Rules* — 16

**CHAPTER 4**
*Applications of Differentiation* — 25

**CHAPTER 5**
*Integrals* — 34

**CHAPTER 6**
*Applications of Integration* — 42

**CHAPTER 7**
*Techniques of Integration* — 47

**CHAPTER 8**
*Further Applications of Integration* — 53

**CHAPTER 9**
*Differential Equations* — 61

**CHAPTER 10**
*Parametric Equations and Polar Coordinates* — 66

**CHAPTER 11**
*Infinite Sequences and Series* — 72

**CHAPTER 12**
*Vectors and the Geometry of Space* — 78

**CHAPTER 13**
*Vector Functions* — 84

**CHAPTER 14**
*Partial Derivatives* — 88

**CHAPTER 15**
*Multiple Integrals* — 96

**CHAPTER 16**
*Vector Calculus* — 102

**CHAPTER 17**
*Second-Order Differential Equations* — 107

**ANSWER KEY** — 112

# TO THE STUDENT

## COMPREHENSIVE

The *MznLnx* Exam Prep series is designed to help you pass your exams. Editors at MznLnx review your textbooks and then prepare these practice exams to help you master the textbook material. Unlike study guides, workbooks, and practice tests provided by the texbook publisher and textbook authors, *MznLnx* gives you **all** of the material in each chapter in exam form, not just samples, so you can be sure to nail your exam.

## MECHANICAL

The MznLnx Exam Prep series creates exams that will help you learn the subject matter as well as test you on your understanding. Each question is designed to help you master the concept. Just working through the exams, you gain an understanding of the subject--its a simple mechanical process that produces success.

## INTEGRATED STUDY GUIDE AND REVIEW

MznLnx is not just a set of exams designed to test you, its also a comprehensive review of the subject content. Each exam question is also a review of the concept, making sure that you will get the answer correct without having to go to other sources of material. You learn as you go! Its the easiest way to pass an exam.

## HUMOR

Studying can be tedious and dry. MznLnx's instructional design includes moderate humor within the exam questions on occassion, to break the tedium and revitalize the brain

## Chapter 1. Functions and Models

1. In mathematics, the _____ of a function is the set of all "output" values produced by that function. Given a function $f: A \to B$, the _____ of $f$, is defined to be the set $\{x \in B : x = f(a) \text{ for some } a \in A\}$.
   a. Range0
   b. Thing
   c. Undefined
   d. Undefined

2. A _____ is a symbolic representation denoting a quantity or expression. It often represents an "unknown" quantity that has the potential to change.
   a. Variable0
   b. Thing
   c. Undefined
   d. Undefined

3. In mathematics, an _____ is any of the arguments, i.e. "inputs", to a function. Thus if we have a function f(x), then x is a _____.
   a. Independent variable0
   b. Thing
   c. Undefined
   d. Undefined

4. In a function the _____, is the variable which is the value, i.e. the "output", of the function.
   a. Thing
   b. Dependent variable0
   c. Undefined
   d. Undefined

5. In mathematics, a _____ is a two-dimensional manifold or surface that is perfectly flat.
   a. Thing
   b. Plane0
   c. Undefined
   d. Undefined

6. In mathematics and the mathematical sciences, a _____ is a fixed, but possibly unspecified, value. This is in contrast to a variable, which is not fixed.

a. Thing
b. Constant0
c. Undefined
d. Undefined

7. _____ is a synonym for information.
a. Data0
b. Thing
c. Undefined
d. Undefined

8. In the scientific method, an _____ (Latin: ex-+-periri, "of (or from) trying"), is a set of actions and observations, performed in the context of solving a particular problem or question, in order to support or falsify a hypothesis or research concerning phenomena.
a. Experiment0
b. Thing
c. Undefined
d. Undefined

9. _____ is a mathematical subject that includes the study of limits, derivatives, integrals, and power series and constitutes a major part of modern university curriculum.
a. Calculus0
b. Thing
c. Undefined
d. Undefined

10. In plane geometry, a _____ is a polygon with four equal sides, four right angles, and parallel opposite sides. In algebra, the _____ of a number is that number multiplied by itself.
a. Square0
b. Thing
c. Undefined
d. Undefined

11. In mathematics, the _____ (or modulus) of a real number is its numerical value without regard to its sign.

## Chapter 1. Functions and Models

a. Absolute value0
b. Thing
c. Undefined
d. Undefined

12. In mathematics, the _____ of a coordinate system is the point where the axes of the system intersect.
    a. Origin0
    b. Thing
    c. Undefined
    d. Undefined

13. In geometry, a _____ is defined as a quadrilateral where all four of its angles are right angles.
    a. Rectangle0
    b. Thing
    c. Undefined
    d. Undefined

14. _____ is the distance around a given two-dimensional object. As a general rule, the _____ of a polygon can always be calculated by adding all the length of the sides together. So, the formula for triangles is P = a + b + c, where a, b and c stand for each side of it. For quadrilaterals the equation is P = a + b + c + d. For equilateral polygons, P = na, where n is the number of sides and a is the side length.
    a. Thing
    b. Perimeter0
    c. Undefined
    d. Undefined

15. _____ means "constancy", i.e. if something retains a certain feature even after we change a way of looking at it, then it is symmetric.
    a. Symmetry0
    b. Thing
    c. Undefined
    d. Undefined

16. _____ is often used to describe the measurement of the steepness, incline, gradient, or grade of a straight line. The _____ is defined as the ratio of the "rise" divided by the "run" between two points on a line, or in other words, the ratio of the altitude change to the horizontal distance between any two points on the line.

## Chapter 1. Functions and Models

   a. Thing
   b. Slope0
   c. Undefined
   d. Undefined

17. In mathematics, an _____, mean, or central tendency of a data set refers to a measure of the "middle" or "expected" value of the data set.
   a. Concept
   b. Average0
   c. Undefined
   d. Undefined

18. In mathematics, a _____ is an expression that is constructed from one or more variables and constants, using only the operations of addition, subtraction, multiplication, and constant positive whole number exponents. is a _____. Note in particular that division by an expression containing a variable is not in general allowed in polynomials. [1]
   a. Polynomial0
   b. Thing
   c. Undefined
   d. Undefined

19. In mathematics, a _____ is a constant multiplicative factor of a certain object. The object can be such things as a variable, a vector, a function, etc. For example, the _____ of $9x^2$ is 9.
   a. Thing
   b. Coefficient0
   c. Undefined
   d. Undefined

20. _____ has many meanings, most of which simply .
   a. Thing
   b. Power0
   c. Undefined
   d. Undefined

21. In mathematics, the multiplicative inverse of a number x, denoted 1/x or $x^{-1}$, is the number which, when multiplied by x, yields 1. The multiplicative inverse of x is also called the _____ of x.

a. Reciprocal0
b. Thing
c. Undefined
d. Undefined

22. In mathematics, _____ is an elementary arithmetic operation. When one of the numbers is a whole number, _____ is the repeated sum of the other number.
a. Multiplication0
b. Thing
c. Undefined
d. Undefined

23. The word _____ comes from the Latin word linearis, which means created by lines.
a. Thing
b. Linear0
c. Undefined
d. Undefined

24. A _____ is a first degree polynomial mathematical function of the form: f(x) = mx + b where m and b are real constants and x is a real variable.
a. Thing
b. Linear function0
c. Undefined
d. Undefined

25. The mathematical concept of a _____ expresses the intuitive idea of deterministic dependence between two quantities, one of which is viewed as primary and the other as secondary. A _____ then is a way to associate a unique output for each input of a specified type, for example, a real number or an element of a given set.
a. Function0
b. Thing
c. Undefined
d. Undefined

26. A _____, scatter diagram or scatter graph is a chart that uses Cartesian coordinates to display values for two variables.

a. Thing
b. Scatter plot0
c. Undefined
d. Undefined

27. In regression analysis, _____, also known as ordinary _____ analysis is a method for linear regression that determines the values of unknown quantities in a statistical model by minimizing the sum of the residuals difference between the predicted and observed values squared.
a. Thing
b. Least squares0
c. Undefined
d. Undefined

28. In Euclidean geometry, a _____ is the set of all points in a plane at a fixed distance, called the radius, from a given point, the center.
a. Circle0
b. Thing
c. Undefined
d. Undefined

29. An _____ is a combination of numbers, operators, grouping symbols and/or free variables and bound variables arranged in a meaningful way which can be evaluated..
a. Thing
b. Expression0
c. Undefined
d. Undefined

30. In elementary algebra, an _____ is a set that contains every real number between two indicated numbers and may contain the two numbers themselves.
a. Interval0
b. Thing
c. Undefined
d. Undefined

31. In mathematics, defined and _____ are used to explain whether or not expressions have meaningful, sensible, and unambiguous values.

a. Thing
b. Undefined0
c. Undefined
d. Undefined

32. In classical geometry, a _____ of a circle or sphere is any line segment from its center to its boundary. By extension, the _____ of a circle or sphere is the length of any such segment. The _____ is half the diameter. In science and engineering the term _____ of curvature is commonly used as a synonym for _____.
    a. Radius0
    b. Thing
    c. Undefined
    d. Undefined

33. In mathematics, a _____ may be described informally as a number that can be given by an infinite decimal representation.
    a. Thing
    b. Real number0
    c. Undefined
    d. Undefined

34. In mathematics, an inequality is a statement about the relative size or order of two objects. For example 14 > 10, or 14 is _____ 10.
    a. Greater than0
    b. Thing
    c. Undefined
    d. Undefined

35. In geometry, a line _____ is a part of a line that is bounded by two end points, and contains every point on the line between its end points.
    a. Concept
    b. Segment0
    c. Undefined
    d. Undefined

36. A _____ is a part of a line that is bounded by two end points, and contains every point on the line between its end points.

a. Line segment0
b. Thing
c. Undefined
d. Undefined

37. _____ is a branch of mathematics concerning the study of structure, relation and quantity.
a. Concept
b. Algebra0
c. Undefined
d. Undefined

38. In sociology and biology a _____ is the collection of people or organisms of a particular species living in a given geographic area or space, usually measured by a census.
a. Thing
b. Population0
c. Undefined
d. Undefined

39. _____ is a subset of a population.
a. Thing
b. Sample0
c. Undefined
d. Undefined

40. In astronomy, geography, geometry and related sciences and contexts, a plane is said to be _____ at a given point if it is locally perpendicular to the gradient of the gravity field, i.e., with the direction of the gravitational force at that point.
a. Horizontal0
b. Thing
c. Undefined
d. Undefined

41. A _____ is one of the basic shapes of geometry: a polygon with three vertices and three sides which are straight line segments.

a. Triangle0
b. Thing
c. Undefined
d. Undefined

42. _____ has one 90° internal angle a right angle.
a. Right triangle0
b. Thing
c. Undefined
d. Undefined

43. The _____ of a right triangle is the triangle's longest side; the side opposite the right angle.
a. Thing
b. Hypotenuse0
c. Undefined
d. Undefined

## Chapter 2. Principles of Problem Solving

1. _____ is a mathematical subject that includes the study of limits, derivatives, integrals, and power series and constitutes a major part of modern university curriculum.
   a. Calculus0
   b. Thing
   c. Undefined
   d. Undefined

2. In plane geometry, a _____ is a polygon with four equal sides, four right angles, and parallel opposite sides. In algebra, the _____ of a number is that number multiplied by itself.
   a. Thing
   b. Square0
   c. Undefined
   d. Undefined

3. In mathematics, an _____, mean, or central tendency of a data set refers to a measure of the "middle" or "expected" value of the data set.
   a. Concept
   b. Average0
   c. Undefined
   d. Undefined

4. In elementary algebra, an _____ is a set that contains every real number between two indicated numbers and may contain the two numbers themselves.
   a. Interval0
   b. Thing
   c. Undefined
   d. Undefined

5. _____ is often used to describe the measurement of the steepness, incline, gradient, or grade of a straight line. The _____ is defined as the ratio of the "rise" divided by the "run" between two points on a line, or in other words, the ratio of the altitude change to the horizontal distance between any two points on the line.
   a. Slope0
   b. Thing
   c. Undefined
   d. Undefined

6. _____ is a synonym for information.

a. Thing
b. Data0
c. Undefined
d. Undefined

7. In mathematics, defined and _____ are used to explain whether or not expressions have meaningful, sensible, and unambiguous values.
a. Thing
b. Undefined0
c. Undefined
d. Undefined

8. In geometry, a _____ is defined as a quadrilateral where all four of its angles are right angles.
a. Rectangle0
b. Thing
c. Undefined
d. Undefined

9. In elementary algebra, a _____ is a polynomial with two terms: the sum of two monomials. It is the simplest kind of polynomial except for a monomial.
a. Thing
b. Binomial0
c. Undefined
d. Undefined

10. _____ has many meanings, most of which simply .
a. Thing
b. Power0
c. Undefined
d. Undefined

11. A _____ is a symbolic representation denoting a quantity or expression. It often represents an "unknown" quantity that has the potential to change.

## Chapter 2. Principles of Problem Solving

   a. Thing
   b. Variable0
   c. Undefined
   d. Undefined

12. In mathematics and the mathematical sciences, a _____ is a fixed, but possibly unspecified, value. This is in contrast to a variable, which is not fixed.
   a. Constant0
   b. Thing
   c. Undefined
   d. Undefined

13. In mathematics, a _____ is an expression that is constructed from one or more variables and constants, using only the operations of addition, subtraction, multiplication, and constant positive whole number exponents. is a _____. Note in particular that division by an expression containing a variable is not in general allowed in polynomials. [1]
   a. Polynomial0
   b. Thing
   c. Undefined
   d. Undefined

14. A _____ is the result of the addition of a set of numbers. The numbers may be natural numbers, complex numbers, matrices, or still more complicated objects. An infinite _____ is a subtle procedure known as a series.
   a. Sum0
   b. Thing
   c. Undefined
   d. Undefined

15. In astronomy, geography, geometry and related sciences and contexts, a plane is said to be _____ at a given point if it is locally perpendicular to the gradient of the gravity field, i.e., with the direction of the gravitational force at that point.
   a. Horizontal0
   b. Thing
   c. Undefined
   d. Undefined

16. A _____ is a numeral used to indicate a count. The most common use of the word today is to name the part of a fraction that tells the number or count of equal parts.

## Chapter 2. Principles of Problem Solving

a. Thing
b. Numerator0
c. Undefined
d. Undefined

17. A _____ is the part of a fraction that tells how many equal parts make up a whole, and which is used in the name of the fraction: "halves", "thirds", "fourths" or "quarters", "fifths" and so on.
a. Concept
b. Denominator0
c. Undefined
d. Undefined

18. A _____ is a quantity that denotes the proportional amount or magnitude of one quantity relative to another.
a. Ratio0
b. Thing
c. Undefined
d. Undefined

19. An _____ is a combination of numbers, operators, grouping symbols and/or free variables and bound variables arranged in a meaningful way which can be evaluated..
a. Thing
b. Expression0
c. Undefined
d. Undefined

20. In mathematics, there are several meanings of _____ depending on the subject.
a. Thing
b. Degree0
c. Undefined
d. Undefined

21. In sociology and biology a _____ is the collection of people or organisms of a particular species living in a given geographic area or space, usually measured by a census.

## Chapter 2. Principles of Problem Solving

a. Population0
b. Thing
c. Undefined
d. Undefined

22. _____ means "constancy", i.e. if something retains a certain feature even after we change a way of looking at it, then it is symmetric.
a. Thing
b. Symmetry0
c. Undefined
d. Undefined

23. In mathematics, a _____ is the result of multiplying, or an expression that identifies factors to be multiplied.
a. Thing
b. Product0
c. Undefined
d. Undefined

24. In mathematics, the _____ of a function is the set of all "output" values produced by that function. Given a function $f : A \to B$, the _____ of $f$, is defined to be the set $\{x \in B : x = f(a) \text{ for some } a \in A\}$.
a. Thing
b. Range0
c. Undefined
d. Undefined

25. In mathematics, the additive inverse, or _____ of a number n is the number that, when added to n, yields zero. The additive inverse of n is denoted −n. For example, 7 is −7, because 7 + (−7) = 0, and the additive inverse of −0.3 is 0.3, because −0.3 + 0.3 = 0.
a. Opposite0
b. Thing
c. Undefined
d. Undefined

26. In mathematics, the _____ of a number n is the number that, when added to n, yields zero. The _____ of n is denoted −n. For example, 7 is −7, because 7 + (−7) = 0, and the _____ of −0.3 is 0.3, because −0.3 + 0.3 = 0.

a. Additive inverse0
b. Thing
c. Undefined
d. Undefined

## Chapter 3. Differentiation Rules

1. In mathematics and the mathematical sciences, a _____ is a fixed, but possibly unspecified, value. This is in contrast to a variable, which is not fixed.
   a. Thing
   b. Constant0
   c. Undefined
   d. Undefined

2. _____ is often used to describe the measurement of the steepness, incline, gradient, or grade of a straight line. The _____ is defined as the ratio of the "rise" divided by the "run" between two points on a line, or in other words, the ratio of the altitude change to the horizontal distance between any two points on the line.
   a. Slope0
   b. Thing
   c. Undefined
   d. Undefined

3. A _____ of a number is the product of that number with any integer.
   a. Multiple0
   b. Thing
   c. Undefined
   d. Undefined

4. A _____ is the result of the addition of a set of numbers. The numbers may be natural numbers, complex numbers, matrices, or still more complicated objects. An infinite _____ is a subtle procedure known as a series.
   a. Sum0
   b. Thing
   c. Undefined
   d. Undefined

5. An _____ is a combination of numbers, operators, grouping symbols and/or free variables and bound variables arranged in a meaningful way which can be evaluated..
   a. Expression0
   b. Thing
   c. Undefined
   d. Undefined

6. In geometry, a _____ is defined as a quadrilateral where all four of its angles are right angles.

a. Thing
b. Rectangle0
c. Undefined
d. Undefined

7. In mathematics, a _____ is the result of multiplying, or an expression that identifies factors to be multiplied.
a. Thing
b. Product0
c. Undefined
d. Undefined

8. _____ is a branch of mathematics concerning the study of structure, relation and quantity.
a. Algebra0
b. Concept
c. Undefined
d. Undefined

9. In mathematics, an _____, mean, or central tendency of a data set refers to a measure of the "middle" or "expected" value of the data set.
a. Average0
b. Concept
c. Undefined
d. Undefined

10. In mathematics, a _____ is the end result of a division problem. It can also be expressed as the number of times the divisor divides into the dividend.
a. Quotient0
b. Thing
c. Undefined
d. Undefined

11. In mathematics, a _____ is an expression that is constructed from one or more variables and constants, using only the operations of addition, subtraction, multiplication, and constant positive whole number exponents. is a _____. Note in particular that division by an expression containing a variable is not in general allowed in polynomials. [1]

a. Thing
b. Polynomial0
c. Undefined
d. Undefined

12. In sociology and biology a _____ is the collection of people or organisms of a particular species living in a given geographic area or space, usually measured by a census.
a. Population0
b. Thing
c. Undefined
d. Undefined

13. _____ is mass m per unit volume V.
a. Density0
b. Thing
c. Undefined
d. Undefined

14. In elementary algebra, an _____ is a set that contains every real number between two indicated numbers and may contain the two numbers themselves.
a. Thing
b. Interval0
c. Undefined
d. Undefined

15. An _____ is a straight line around which a geometric figure can be rotated.
a. Thing
b. Axis0
c. Undefined
d. Undefined

16. _____ is the distance around a given two-dimensional object. As a general rule, the _____ of a polygon can always be calculated by adding all the length of the sides together. So, the formula for triangles is P = a + b + c, where a, b and c stand for each side of it. For quadrilaterals the equation is P = a + b + c + d. For equilateral polygons, P = na, where n is the number of sides and a is the side length.

a. Perimeter0
b. Thing
c. Undefined
d. Undefined

17. In plane geometry, a _____ is a polygon with four equal sides, four right angles, and parallel opposite sides. In algebra, the _____ of a number is that number multiplied by itself.
a. Thing
b. Square0
c. Undefined
d. Undefined

18. In Euclidean geometry, a _____ is the set of all points in a plane at a fixed distance, called the radius, from a given point, the center.
a. Thing
b. Circle0
c. Undefined
d. Undefined

19. The _____ is the distance around a closed curve. _____ is a kind of perimeter.
a. Circumference0
b. Thing
c. Undefined
d. Undefined

20. In classical geometry, a _____ of a circle or sphere is any line segment from its center to its boundary. By extension, the _____ of a circle or sphere is the length of any such segment. The _____ is half the diameter. In science and engineering the term _____ of curvature is commonly used as a synonym for _____.
a. Thing
b. Radius0
c. Undefined
d. Undefined

21. _____ is a subset of a population.

a. Sample0
b. Thing
c. Undefined
d. Undefined

22. _____ is a synonym for information.
a. Data0
b. Thing
c. Undefined
d. Undefined

23. In statistics the _____ of an event i is the number $n_i$ of times the event occurred in the experiment or the study. These frequencies are often graphically represented in histograms.
a. Concept
b. Frequency0
c. Undefined
d. Undefined

24. In mathematics, a _____ is a constant multiplicative factor of a certain object. The object can be such things as a variable, a vector, a function, etc. For example, the _____ of $9x^2$ is 9.
a. Thing
b. Coefficient0
c. Undefined
d. Undefined

25. In mathematics, a _____ is a two-dimensional manifold or surface that is perfectly flat.
a. Thing
b. Plane0
c. Undefined
d. Undefined

26. _____ has many meanings, most of which simply .

## Chapter 3. Differentiation Rules 21

   a. Thing
   b. Power0
   c. Undefined
   d. Undefined

27. A _____ is a symbolic representation denoting a quantity or expression. It often represents an "unknown" quantity that has the potential to change.
   a. Thing
   b. Variable0
   c. Undefined
   d. Undefined

28. A _____ is the part of a fraction that tells how many equal parts make up a whole, and which is used in the name of the fraction: "halves", "thirds", "fourths" or "quarters", "fifths" and so on.
   a. Denominator0
   b. Concept
   c. Undefined
   d. Undefined

29. In mathematics, the _____ of a coordinate system is the point where the axes of the system intersect.
   a. Thing
   b. Origin0
   c. Undefined
   d. Undefined

30. In mathematics, an _____ is any of the arguments, i.e. "inputs", to a function. Thus if we have a function f(x), then x is a _____.
   a. Thing
   b. Independent variable0
   c. Undefined
   d. Undefined

31. In mathematics, the _____ (or modulus) of a real number is its numerical value without regard to its sign.

a. Absolute value0
b. Thing
c. Undefined
d. Undefined

32. In mathematics, the _____ of a function is the set of all "output" values produced by that function. Given a function $f: A \to B$, the _____ of $f$, is defined to be the set $\{x \in B : x = f(a) \text{ for some } a \in A\}$.
    a. Range0
    b. Thing
    c. Undefined
    d. Undefined

33. In geometry, a _____ (Greek words diairo = divide and metro = measure) of a circle is any straight line segment that passes through the centre and whose endpoints are on the circular boundary, or, in more modern usage, the length of such a line segment. When using the word in the more modern sense, one speaks of the _____ rather than a _____, because all diameters of a circle have the same length. This length is twice the radius. The _____ of a circle is also the longest chord that the circle has.
    a. Thing
    b. Diameter0
    c. Undefined
    d. Undefined

34. A _____ is a quadrilateral, which is defined as a shape with four sides, which has a pair of parallel sides.
    a. Trapezoid0
    b. Thing
    c. Undefined
    d. Undefined

35. _____ is a mathematical subject that includes the study of limits, derivatives, integrals, and power series and constitutes a major part of modern university curriculum.
    a. Thing
    b. Calculus0
    c. Undefined
    d. Undefined

36. _____ is the estimation of a physical quantity such as distance, energy, temperature, or time.

## Chapter 3. Differentiation Rules

a. Measurement0
b. Thing
c. Undefined
d. Undefined

37. In botany, _____ are above-ground plant organs specialized for photosynthesis. Their characteristics are typically analyzed by using Fiobonacci's sequences.
    a. Thing
    b. Leaves0
    c. Undefined
    d. Undefined

38. In astronomy, geography, geometry and related sciences and contexts, a plane is said to be _____ at a given point if it is locally perpendicular to the gradient of the gravity field, i.e., with the direction of the gravitational force at that point.
    a. Thing
    b. Horizontal0
    c. Undefined
    d. Undefined

39. In geometry, a line _____ is a part of a line that is bounded by two end points, and contains every point on the line between its end points.
    a. Segment0
    b. Concept
    c. Undefined
    d. Undefined

40. A _____ is a part of a line that is bounded by two end points, and contains every point on the line between its end points.
    a. Thing
    b. Line segment0
    c. Undefined
    d. Undefined

41. A _____ given two distinct points A and B on the _____, is the set of points C on the line containing points A and B such that A is not strictly between C and B.

a. Ray0
b. Thing
c. Undefined
d. Undefined

## Chapter 4. Applications of Differentiation

1. In elementary algebra, an _____ is a set that contains every real number between two indicated numbers and may contain the two numbers themselves.
   a. Interval0
   b. Thing
   c. Undefined
   d. Undefined

2. In mathematics, the _____ of a function is the set of all "output" values produced by that function. Given a function $f : A \to B$, the _____ of $f$, is defined to be the set $\{x \in B : x = f(a) \text{ for some } a \in A\}$.
   a. Thing
   b. Range0
   c. Undefined
   d. Undefined

3. _____ is a mathematical subject that includes the study of limits, derivatives, integrals, and power series and constitutes a major part of modern university curriculum.
   a. Calculus0
   b. Thing
   c. Undefined
   d. Undefined

4. In mathematics, a _____ is the result of multiplying, or an expression that identifies factors to be multiplied.
   a. Thing
   b. Product0
   c. Undefined
   d. Undefined

5. In geometry, a _____ is defined as a quadrilateral where all four of its angles are right angles.
   a. Thing
   b. Rectangle0
   c. Undefined
   d. Undefined

6. In mathematics, a _____ is a constant multiplicative factor of a certain object. The object can be such things as a variable, a vector, a function, etc. For example, the _____ of $9x^2$ is 9.

## Chapter 4. Applications of Differentiation

a. Coefficient0
b. Thing
c. Undefined
d. Undefined

7. In mathematics and the mathematical sciences, a _____ is a fixed, but possibly unspecified, value. This is in contrast to a variable, which is not fixed.
   a. Constant0
   b. Thing
   c. Undefined
   d. Undefined

8. In mathematics, a _____ is a two-dimensional manifold or surface that is perfectly flat.
   a. Plane0
   b. Thing
   c. Undefined
   d. Undefined

9. In mathematics, a _____ is an expression that is constructed from one or more variables and constants, using only the operations of addition, subtraction, multiplication, and constant positive whole number exponents. is a _____. Note in particular that division by an expression containing a variable is not in general allowed in polynomials. [1]
   a. Polynomial0
   b. Thing
   c. Undefined
   d. Undefined

10. In classical geometry, a _____ of a circle or sphere is any line segment from its center to its boundary. By extension, the _____ of a circle or sphere is the length of any such segment. The _____ is half the diameter. In science and engineering the term _____ of curvature is commonly used as a synonym for _____.
    a. Thing
    b. Radius0
    c. Undefined
    d. Undefined

11. In mathematics, an inequality is a statement about the relative size or order of two objects. For example 14 > 10, or 14 is _____ 10.

a. Greater than0
b. Thing
c. Undefined
d. Undefined

12. _____ is a measure of difference for interval and ratio variables between the observed value and the mean.
a. Deviation0
b. Thing
c. Undefined
d. Undefined

13. A _____ given two distinct points A and B on the _____, is the set of points C on the line containing points A and B such that A is not strictly between C and B.
a. Thing
b. Ray0
c. Undefined
d. Undefined

14. In botany, _____ are above-ground plant organs specialized for photosynthesis. Their characteristics are typically analyzed by using Fiobonacci's sequences.
a. Thing
b. Leaves0
c. Undefined
d. Undefined

15. The _____, the average in everyday English, which is also called the arithmetic _____ (and is distinguished from the geometric _____ or harmonic _____). The average is also called the sample _____. The expected value of a random variable, which is also called the population _____.
a. Mean0
b. Thing
c. Undefined
d. Undefined

16. In mathematics, a _____ may be described informally as a number that can be given by an infinite decimal representation.

## Chapter 4. Applications of Differentiation

   a. Real number0
   b. Thing
   c. Undefined
   d. Undefined

17. _____ is often used to describe the measurement of the steepness, incline, gradient, or grade of a straight line. The _____ is defined as the ratio of the "rise" divided by the "run" between two points on a line, or in other words, the ratio of the altitude change to the horizontal distance between any two points on the line.
   a. Slope0
   b. Thing
   c. Undefined
   d. Undefined

18. An _____ is a combination of numbers, operators, grouping symbols and/or free variables and bound variables arranged in a meaningful way which can be evaluated..
   a. Expression0
   b. Thing
   c. Undefined
   d. Undefined

19. The plus and _____ signs are mathematical symbols used to represent the notions of positive and negative as well as the operations of addition and subtraction.
   a. Minus0
   b. Thing
   c. Undefined
   d. Undefined

20. In sociology and biology a _____ is the collection of people or organisms of a particular species living in a given geographic area or space, usually measured by a census.
   a. Thing
   b. Population0
   c. Undefined
   d. Undefined

21. A _____ is the part of a fraction that tells how many equal parts make up a whole, and which is used in the name of the fraction: "halves", "thirds", "fourths" or "quarters", "fifths" and so on.

## Chapter 4. Applications of Differentiation

a. Denominator0
b. Concept
c. Undefined
d. Undefined

22. A _____ is a numeral used to indicate a count. The most common use of the word today is to name the part of a fraction that tells the number or count of equal parts.
   a. Thing
   b. Numerator0
   c. Undefined
   d. Undefined

23. In mathematics, a _____ is the end result of a division problem. It can also be expressed as the number of times the divisor divides into the dividend.
   a. Thing
   b. Quotient0
   c. Undefined
   d. Undefined

24. _____ means "constancy", i.e. if something retains a certain feature even after we change a way of looking at it, then it is symmetric.
   a. Thing
   b. Symmetry0
   c. Undefined
   d. Undefined

25. In mathematics, the _____ of a coordinate system is the point where the axes of the system intersect.
   a. Origin0
   b. Thing
   c. Undefined
   d. Undefined

26. In geometry, an _____ is a point at which a line segment or ray terminates.

a. Endpoint0
b. Thing
c. Undefined
d. Undefined

27. In plane geometry, a _____ is a polygon with four equal sides, four right angles, and parallel opposite sides. In algebra, the _____ of a number is that number multiplied by itself.
    a. Square0
    b. Thing
    c. Undefined
    d. Undefined

28. In statistics the _____ of an event i is the number $n_i$ of times the event occurred in the experiment or the study. These frequencies are often graphically represented in histograms.
    a. Frequency0
    b. Concept
    c. Undefined
    d. Undefined

29. In Euclidean geometry, a _____ is the set of all points in a plane at a fixed distance, called the radius, from a given point, the center.
    a. Thing
    b. Circle0
    c. Undefined
    d. Undefined

30. A _____ is a symbolic representation denoting a quantity or expression. It often represents an "unknown" quantity that has the potential to change.
    a. Thing
    b. Variable0
    c. Undefined
    d. Undefined

## Chapter 4. Applications of Differentiation

31. _____ is the distance around a given two-dimensional object. As a general rule, the _____ of a polygon can always be calculated by adding all the length of the sides together. So, the formula for triangles is P = a + b + c, where a, b and c stand for each side of it. For quadrilaterals the equation is P = a + b + c + d. For equilateral polygons, P = na, where n is the number of sides and a is the side length.
    a. Perimeter0
    b. Thing
    c. Undefined
    d. Undefined

32. In geometry, a _____ (Greek words diairo = divide and metro = measure) of a circle is any straight line segment that passes through the centre and whose endpoints are on the circular boundary, or, in more modern usage, the length of such a line segment. When using the word in the more modern sense, one speaks of the _____ rather than a _____, because all diameters of a circle have the same length. This length is twice the radius. The _____ of a circle is also the longest chord that the circle has.
    a. Thing
    b. Diameter0
    c. Undefined
    d. Undefined

33. A _____ is one of the basic shapes of geometry: a polygon with three vertices and three sides which are straight line segments.
    a. Thing
    b. Triangle0
    c. Undefined
    d. Undefined

34. In geometry, an _____ polygon is a polygon which has all sides of the same length.
    a. Thing
    b. Equilateral0
    c. Undefined
    d. Undefined

35. An _____ is a triangle in which all sides are of equal length.

## Chapter 4. Applications of Differentiation

   a. Thing
   b. Equilateral triangle0
   c. Undefined
   d. Undefined

36. A _____ is a polygon with six edges and six vertices.
   a. Hexagon0
   b. Thing
   c. Undefined
   d. Undefined

37. A _____ is a quantity that denotes the proportional amount or magnitude of one quantity relative to another.
   a. Ratio0
   b. Thing
   c. Undefined
   d. Undefined

38. _____ is the middle point of a line segment.
   a. Thing
   b. Midpoint0
   c. Undefined
   d. Undefined

39. In Euclidean geometry, a uniform _____ is a linear transformation that enlargers or diminishes objects, and whose _____ factor is the same in all directions. This is also called homothethy.
   a. Thing
   b. Scale0
   c. Undefined
   d. Undefined

40. In mathematics, an _____, mean, or central tendency of a data set refers to a measure of the "middle" or "expected" value of the data set.

a. Concept
b. Average0
c. Undefined
d. Undefined

41. _____ is a branch of mathematics concerning the study of structure, relation and quantity.
a. Concept
b. Algebra0
c. Undefined
d. Undefined

42. _____ is mass m per unit volume V.
a. Thing
b. Density0
c. Undefined
d. Undefined

43. The _____ of a right triangle is the triangle's longest side; the side opposite the right angle.
a. Thing
b. Hypotenuse0
c. Undefined
d. Undefined

## Chapter 5. Integrals

1. _____ is a mathematical subject that includes the study of limits, derivatives, integrals, and power series and constitutes a major part of modern university curriculum.
    a. Calculus0
    b. Thing
    c. Undefined
    d. Undefined

2. The _____ of a function is an extension of the concept of a sum, and are identified or found through the use of integration.
    a. Thing
    b. Integral0
    c. Undefined
    d. Undefined

3. A _____ is one of the basic shapes of geometry: a polygon with three vertices and three sides which are straight line segments.
    a. Thing
    b. Triangle0
    c. Undefined
    d. Undefined

4. In geometry a _____ is a plane figure that is bounded by a closed path or circuit, composed of a finite number of sequential line segments.
    a. Polygon0
    b. Thing
    c. Undefined
    d. Undefined

5. In geometry, an _____ is a point at which a line segment or ray terminates.
    a. Thing
    b. Endpoint0
    c. Undefined
    d. Undefined

6. In geometry, a _____ is defined as a quadrilateral where all four of its angles are right angles.

a. Thing
b. Rectangle0
c. Undefined
d. Undefined

7. _____ is a subset of a population.
a. Sample0
b. Thing
c. Undefined
d. Undefined

8. A _____ is the result of the addition of a set of numbers. The numbers may be natural numbers, complex numbers, matrices, or still more complicated objects. An infinite _____ is a subtle procedure known as a series.
a. Sum0
b. Thing
c. Undefined
d. Undefined

9. In elementary algebra, an _____ is a set that contains every real number between two indicated numbers and may contain the two numbers themselves.
a. Thing
b. Interval0
c. Undefined
d. Undefined

10. _____ is a synonym for information.
a. Data0
b. Thing
c. Undefined
d. Undefined

11. _____ is a branch of mathematics concerning the study of structure, relation and quantity.

## Chapter 5. Integrals

a. Concept
b. Algebra0
c. Undefined
d. Undefined

12. In Euclidean geometry, a _____ is the set of all points in a plane at a fixed distance, called the radius, from a given point, the center.
a. Thing
b. Circle0
c. Undefined
d. Undefined

13. An _____ is a combination of numbers, operators, grouping symbols and/or free variables and bound variables arranged in a meaningful way which can be evaluated..
a. Thing
b. Expression0
c. Undefined
d. Undefined

14. In classical geometry, a _____ of a circle or sphere is any line segment from its center to its boundary. By extension, the _____ of a circle or sphere is the length of any such segment. The _____ is half the diameter. In science and engineering the term _____ of curvature is commonly used as a synonym for _____.
a. Thing
b. Radius0
c. Undefined
d. Undefined

15. _____ is the middle point of a line segment.
a. Thing
b. Midpoint0
c. Undefined
d. Undefined

16. In mathematics and the mathematical sciences, a _____ is a fixed, but possibly unspecified, value. This is in contrast to a variable, which is not fixed.

a. Thing
b. Constant0
c. Undefined
d. Undefined


17. The _____, the average in everyday English, which is also called the arithmetic _____ (and is distinguished from the geometric _____ or harmonic _____). The average is also called the sample _____. The expected value of a random variable, which is also called the population _____.
   a. Mean0
   b. Thing
   c. Undefined
   d. Undefined


18. _____ is often used to describe the measurement of the steepness, incline, gradient, or grade of a straight line. The _____ is defined as the ratio of the "rise" divided by the "run" between two points on a line, or in other words, the ratio of the altitude change to the horizontal distance between any two points on the line.
   a. Thing
   b. Slope0
   c. Undefined
   d. Undefined


19. A _____ is traditionally an infinitesimally small change in a variable.
   a. Differential0
   b. Thing
   c. Undefined
   d. Undefined


20. _____, a field in mathematics, is the study of how functions change when their inputs change. The primary object of study in _____ is the derivative.
   a. Differential calculus0
   b. Thing
   c. Undefined
   d. Undefined


21. A _____ is a symbolic representation denoting a quantity or expression. It often represents an "unknown" quantity that has the potential to change.

## Chapter 5. Integrals

   a. Thing
   b. Variable0
   c. Undefined
   d. Undefined

22. _____ is a mathematical science pertaining to the collection, analysis, interpretation or explanation, and presentation of data. It is applicable to a wide variety of academic disciplines, from the physical and social sciences to the humanities.
   a. Statistics0
   b. Thing
   c. Undefined
   d. Undefined

23.   In mathematics, the _____ of a coordinate system is the point where the axes of the system intersect.
   a. Thing
   b. Origin0
   c. Undefined
   d. Undefined

24.   In mathematics, a _____ is the result of multiplying, or an expression that identifies factors to be multiplied.
   a. Thing
   b. Product0
   c. Undefined
   d. Undefined

25.   In mathematical analysis, _____ are objects which generalize functions and probability distributions.
   a. Thing
   b. Distribution0
   c. Undefined
   d. Undefined

26.   In mathematics, a _____ is a constant multiplicative factor of a certain object. The object can be such things as a variable, a vector, a function, etc. For example, the _____ of $9x^2$ is 9.

a. Coefficient0
b. Thing
c. Undefined
d. Undefined

27. A _____ is a quantity that denotes the proportional amount or magnitude of one quantity relative to another.
a. Thing
b. Ratio0
c. Undefined
d. Undefined

28. In mathematics, a _____ is an expression that is constructed from one or more variables and constants, using only the operations of addition, subtraction, multiplication, and constant positive whole number exponents. is a _____. Note in particular that division by an expression containing a variable is not in general allowed in polynomials. [1]
a. Thing
b. Polynomial0
c. Undefined
d. Undefined

29. In mathematics, the _____ of a function is the set of all "output" values produced by that function. Given a function $f : A \to B$, the _____ of $f$, is defined to be the set $\{x \in B : x = f(a) \text{ for some } a \in A\}$.
a. Thing
b. Range0
c. Undefined
d. Undefined

30. _____ means "constancy", i.e. if something retains a certain feature even after we change a way of looking at it, then it is symmetric.
a. Thing
b. Symmetry0
c. Undefined
d. Undefined

31. An _____ is a straight line around which a geometric figure can be rotated.

a. Thing
b. Axis0
c. Undefined
d. Undefined

32. In mathematics, a _____ number is a number which can be expressed as a ratio of two integers. Non-integer _____ numbers (commonly called fractions) are usually written as the vulgar fraction a / b, where b is not zero.
   a. Rational0
   b. Thing
   c. Undefined
   d. Undefined

33. In sociology and biology a _____ is the collection of people or organisms of a particular species living in a given geographic area or space, usually measured by a census.
   a. Thing
   b. Population0
   c. Undefined
   d. Undefined

34. In mathematics, a _____ may be described informally as a number that can be given by an infinite decimal representation.
   a. Real number0
   b. Thing
   c. Undefined
   d. Undefined

35. In plane geometry, a _____ is a polygon with four equal sides, four right angles, and parallel opposite sides. In algebra, the _____ of a number is that number multiplied by itself.
   a. Square0
   b. Thing
   c. Undefined
   d. Undefined

36. In elementary algebra, a _____ is a polynomial with two terms: the sum of two monomials. It is the simplest kind of polynomial except for a monomial.

a. Thing
b. Binomial0
c. Undefined
d. Undefined

# Chapter 6. Applications of Integration

1. In geometry, a _____ is defined as a quadrilateral where all four of its angles are right angles.
   a. Thing
   b. Rectangle0
   c. Undefined
   d. Undefined

2. _____ is the middle point of a line segment.
   a. Thing
   b. Midpoint0
   c. Undefined
   d. Undefined

3. In elementary algebra, an _____ is a set that contains every real number between two indicated numbers and may contain the two numbers themselves.
   a. Interval0
   b. Thing
   c. Undefined
   d. Undefined

4. In Euclidean geometry, an _____ is a closed segment of a differentiable curve in the two-dimensional plane; for example, a circular _____ is a segment of a circle.
   a. Concept
   b. Arc0
   c. Undefined
   d. Undefined

5. In Euclidean geometry, a _____ is the set of all points in a plane at a fixed distance, called the radius, from a given point, the center.
   a. Thing
   b. Circle0
   c. Undefined
   d. Undefined

6. In classical geometry, a _____ of a circle or sphere is any line segment from its center to its boundary. By extension, the _____ of a circle or sphere is the length of any such segment. The _____ is half the diameter. In science and engineering the term _____ of curvature is commonly used as a synonym for _____.

## Chapter 6. Applications of Integration

   a. Radius0
   b. Thing
   c. Undefined
   d. Undefined

7. An _____ is a straight line around which a geometric figure can be rotated.
   a. Axis0
   b. Thing
   c. Undefined
   d. Undefined

8. In mathematics, a _____ is a two-dimensional manifold or surface that is perfectly flat.
   a. Thing
   b. Plane0
   c. Undefined
   d. Undefined

9. In geometry, a _____ (Greek words diairo = divide and metro = measure) of a circle is any straight line segment that passes through the centre and whose endpoints are on the circular boundary, or, in more modern usage, the length of such a line segment. When using the word in the more modern sense, one speaks of the _____ rather than a _____, because all diameters of a circle have the same length. This length is twice the radius. The _____ of a circle is also the longest chord that the circle has.
   a. Thing
   b. Diameter0
   c. Undefined
   d. Undefined

10. In plane geometry, a _____ is a polygon with four equal sides, four right angles, and parallel opposite sides. In algebra, the _____ of a number is that number multiplied by itself.
    a. Square0
    b. Thing
    c. Undefined
    d. Undefined

11. In mathematics and the mathematical sciences, a _____ is a fixed, but possibly unspecified, value. This is in contrast to a variable, which is not fixed.

## Chapter 6. Applications of Integration

    a. Constant0
    b. Thing
    c. Undefined
    d. Undefined

12. In mathematics, an _____, mean, or central tendency of a data set refers to a measure of the "middle" or "expected" value of the data set.
    a. Average0
    b. Concept
    c. Undefined
    d. Undefined

13. A _____ is the result of the addition of a set of numbers. The numbers may be natural numbers, complex numbers, matrices, or still more complicated objects. An infinite _____ is a subtle procedure known as a series.
    a. Thing
    b. Sum0
    c. Undefined
    d. Undefined

14. The _____ is the distance around a closed curve. _____ is a kind of perimeter.
    a. Circumference0
    b. Thing
    c. Undefined
    d. Undefined

15. In mathematics a _____ is a function which defines a distance between elements of a set.
    a. Metric0
    b. Thing
    c. Undefined
    d. Undefined

16. The _____ is a decimalized system of measurement based on the metre and the gram.

a. Metric system0
b. Concept
c. Undefined
d. Undefined

17. In mathematics, a _____ is the result of multiplying, or an expression that identifies factors to be multiplied.
a. Product0
b. Thing
c. Undefined
d. Undefined

18. _____ is mass m per unit volume V.
a. Thing
b. Density0
c. Undefined
d. Undefined

19. _____ is a mathematical subject that includes the study of limits, derivatives, integrals, and power series and constitutes a major part of modern university curriculum.
a. Calculus0
b. Thing
c. Undefined
d. Undefined

20. The _____, the average in everyday English, which is also called the arithmetic _____ (and is distinguished from the geometric _____ or harmonic _____). The average is also called the sample _____. The expected value of a random variable, which is also called the population _____.
a. Mean0
b. Thing
c. Undefined
d. Undefined

21. A _____ is one of the basic shapes of geometry: a polygon with three vertices and three sides which are straight line segments.

a. Triangle0
b. Thing
c. Undefined
d. Undefined


22. In geometry, an _____ polygon is a polygon which has all sides of the same length.
a. Thing
b. Equilateral0
c. Undefined
d. Undefined


23. An _____ is a triangle in which all sides are of equal length.
a. Equilateral triangle0
b. Thing
c. Undefined
d. Undefined

## Chapter 7. Techniques of Integration

1. In mathematics, a _____ is the result of multiplying, or an expression that identifies factors to be multiplied.
    a. Thing
    b. Product0
    c. Undefined
    d. Undefined

2. In geometry, a _____ is defined as a quadrilateral where all four of its angles are right angles.
    a. Rectangle0
    b. Thing
    c. Undefined
    d. Undefined

3. In plane geometry, a _____ is a polygon with four equal sides, four right angles, and parallel opposite sides. In algebra, the _____ of a number is that number multiplied by itself.
    a. Thing
    b. Square0
    c. Undefined
    d. Undefined

4. In mathematics, factorization (British English: factorisation) or factoring is the decomposition of an object (for example, a number, a polynomial, or a matrix) into a product of other objects, or _____, which when multiplied together give the original.
    a. Factors0
    b. Thing
    c. Undefined
    d. Undefined

5. _____ has many meanings, most of which simply .
    a. Power0
    b. Thing
    c. Undefined
    d. Undefined

6. In mathematics, an _____, mean, or central tendency of a data set refers to a measure of the "middle" or "expected" value of the data set.

a. Average0
b. Concept
c. Undefined
d. Undefined

7. In mathematics, a _____ of a number x is a number r such that $r^2$ = x, or in words, a number r whose square (the result of multiplying the number by itself) is x.
a. Thing
b. Square root0
c. Undefined
d. Undefined

8. In mathematics, a _____ of a complex-valued function f is a member x of the domain of f such that f(x) vanishes at x, that is, x : f (x) = 0.
a. Root0
b. Thing
c. Undefined
d. Undefined

9. The _____ are the only integral domain whose positive elements are well-ordered, and in which order is preserved by addition. Like the natural numbers, the _____ form a countably infinite set. The set of all _____ is usually denoted in mathematics by a boldface Z .
a. Integers0
b. Thing
c. Undefined
d. Undefined

10. In Euclidean geometry, a _____ is the set of all points in a plane at a fixed distance, called the radius, from a given point, the center.
a. Thing
b. Circle0
c. Undefined
d. Undefined

11. In mathematics, a _____ is a constant multiplicative factor of a certain object. The object can be such things as a variable, a vector, a function, etc. For example, the _____ of $9x^2$ is 9.

## Chapter 7. Techniques of Integration

 a. Coefficient0
 b. Thing
 c. Undefined
 d. Undefined

12. A _____ is the result of the addition of a set of numbers. The numbers may be natural numbers, complex numbers, matrices, or still more complicated objects. An infinite _____ is a subtle procedure known as a series.
 a. Thing
 b. Sum0
 c. Undefined
 d. Undefined

13. A _____ is one of the basic shapes of geometry: a polygon with three vertices and three sides which are straight line segments.
 a. Thing
 b. Triangle0
 c. Undefined
 d. Undefined

14. A _____ is the part of a fraction that tells how many equal parts make up a whole, and which is used in the name of the fraction: "halves", "thirds", "fourths" or "quarters", "fifths" and so on.
 a. Denominator0
 b. Concept
 c. Undefined
 d. Undefined

15. In mathematics and the mathematical sciences, a _____ is a fixed, but possibly unspecified, value. This is in contrast to a variable, which is not fixed.
 a. Thing
 b. Constant0
 c. Undefined
 d. Undefined

16. An _____ is a combination of numbers, operators, grouping symbols and/or free variables and bound variables arranged in a meaningful way which can be evaluated..

a. Thing
b. Expression0
c. Undefined
d. Undefined

17. In sociology and biology a _____ is the collection of people or organisms of a particular species living in a given geographic area or space, usually measured by a census.
a. Population0
b. Thing
c. Undefined
d. Undefined

18. _____ has one 90° internal angle a right angle.
a. Thing
b. Right triangle0
c. Undefined
d. Undefined

19. _____ is a branch of mathematics concerning the study of structure, relation and quantity.
a. Concept
b. Algebra0
c. Undefined
d. Undefined

20. The _____, the average in everyday English, which is also called the arithmetic _____ (and is distinguished from the geometric _____ or harmonic _____). The average is also called the sample _____. The expected value of a random variable, which is also called the population _____.
a. Mean0
b. Thing
c. Undefined
d. Undefined

21. In elementary algebra, a _____ is a polynomial with two terms: the sum of two monomials. It is the simplest kind of polynomial except for a monomial.

a. Binomial0
b. Thing
c. Undefined
d. Undefined

22. _____ is the middle point of a line segment.
a. Thing
b. Midpoint0
c. Undefined
d. Undefined

23. _____ is a mathematical subject that includes the study of limits, derivatives, integrals, and power series and constitutes a major part of modern university curriculum.
a. Calculus0
b. Thing
c. Undefined
d. Undefined

24. A _____ is a quadrilateral, which is defined as a shape with four sides, which has a pair of parallel sides.
a. Thing
b. Trapezoid0
c. Undefined
d. Undefined

25. In elementary algebra, an _____ is a set that contains every real number between two indicated numbers and may contain the two numbers themselves.
a. Interval0
b. Thing
c. Undefined
d. Undefined

26. _____ is mass m per unit volume V.

## Chapter 7. Techniques of Integration

   a. Density0
   b. Thing
   c. Undefined
   d. Undefined

27. In mathematics, a _____ may be described informally as a number that can be given by an infinite decimal representation.
   a. Thing
   b. Real number0
   c. Undefined
   d. Undefined

28. In mathematics, a _____ is an expression that is constructed from one or more variables and constants, using only the operations of addition, subtraction, multiplication, and constant positive whole number exponents. is a _____. Note in particular that division by an expression containing a variable is not in general allowed in polynomials. [1]
   a. Thing
   b. Polynomial0
   c. Undefined
   d. Undefined

## Chapter 8. Further Applications of Integration

1. In Euclidean geometry, an _____ is a closed segment of a differentiable curve in the two-dimensional plane; for example, a circular _____ is a segment of a circle.
    a. Arc0
    b. Concept
    c. Undefined
    d. Undefined

2. In Euclidean geometry, a _____ is the set of all points in a plane at a fixed distance, called the radius, from a given point, the center.
    a. Circle0
    b. Thing
    c. Undefined
    d. Undefined

3. An _____ is a straight line around which a geometric figure can be rotated.
    a. Thing
    b. Axis0
    c. Undefined
    d. Undefined

4. In geometry a _____ is a plane figure that is bounded by a closed path or circuit, composed of a finite number of sequential line segments.
    a. Polygon0
    b. Thing
    c. Undefined
    d. Undefined

5. In geometry, a line _____ is a part of a line that is bounded by two end points, and contains every point on the line between its end points.
    a. Concept
    b. Segment0
    c. Undefined
    d. Undefined

6. A _____ is a part of a line that is bounded by two end points, and contains every point on the line between its end points.

## Chapter 8. Further Applications of Integration

   a. Thing
   b. Line segment0
   c. Undefined
   d. Undefined

7. A _____ is a symbolic representation denoting a quantity or expression. It often represents an "unknown" quantity that has the potential to change.
   a. Thing
   b. Variable0
   c. Undefined
   d. Undefined

8. In geometry, a _____ (Greek words diairo = divide and metro = measure) of a circle is any straight line segment that passes through the centre and whose endpoints are on the circular boundary, or, in more modern usage, the length of such a line segment. When using the word in the more modern sense, one speaks of the _____ rather than a _____, because all diameters of a circle have the same length. This length is twice the radius. The _____ of a circle is also the longest chord that the circle has.
   a. Thing
   b. Diameter0
   c. Undefined
   d. Undefined

9. _____ is mass m per unit volume V.
   a. Thing
   b. Density0
   c. Undefined
   d. Undefined

10. In mathematics, a _____ is a two-dimensional manifold or surface that is perfectly flat.
   a. Plane0
   b. Thing
   c. Undefined
   d. Undefined

## Chapter 8. Further Applications of Integration

11. In classical geometry, a _____ of a circle or sphere is any line segment from its center to its boundary. By extension, the _____ of a circle or sphere is the length of any such segment. The _____ is half the diameter. In science and engineering the term _____ of curvature is commonly used as a synonym for _____.
    a. Radius0
    b. Thing
    c. Undefined
    d. Undefined

12. In mathematics, the additive inverse, or _____ of a number n is the number that, when added to n, yields zero. The additive inverse of n is denoted −n. For example, 7 is −7, because 7 + (−7) = 0, and the additive inverse of −0.3 is 0.3, because −0.3 + 0.3 = 0.
    a. Opposite0
    b. Thing
    c. Undefined
    d. Undefined

13. In mathematics, the _____ of a number n is the number that, when added to n, yields zero. The _____ of n is denoted −n. For example, 7 is −7, because 7 + (−7) = 0, and the _____ of −0.3 is 0.3, because −0.3 + 0.3 = 0.
    a. Thing
    b. Additive inverse0
    c. Undefined
    d. Undefined

14. In mathematics, a _____ is the result of multiplying, or an expression that identifies factors to be multiplied.
    a. Thing
    b. Product0
    c. Undefined
    d. Undefined

15. _____ is the chance that something is likely to happen or be the case.
    a. Probability0
    b. Thing
    c. Undefined
    d. Undefined

## Chapter 8. Further Applications of Integration

16. In mathematics and the mathematical sciences, a _____ is a fixed, but possibly unspecified, value. This is in contrast to a variable, which is not fixed.
    a. Constant0
    b. Thing
    c. Undefined
    d. Undefined

17. _____ is a mathematical subject that includes the study of limits, derivatives, integrals, and power series and constitutes a major part of modern university curriculum.
    a. Calculus0
    b. Thing
    c. Undefined
    d. Undefined

18. A _____ function is a function for which, intuitively, small changes in the input result in small changes in the output.
    a. Continuous0
    b. Event
    c. Undefined
    d. Undefined

19. _____ is a quantity whose values are random and to which a probability distribution is assigned.
    a. Random variable0
    b. Thing
    c. Undefined
    d. Undefined

20. _____ is a function that represents a probability distribution in terms of integrals.
    a. Probability density function0
    b. Thing
    c. Undefined
    d. Undefined

21. The mathematical concept of a _____ expresses the intuitive idea of deterministic dependence between two quantities, one of which is viewed as primary and the other as secondary. A _____ then is a way to associate a unique output for each input of a specified type, for example, a real number or an element of a given set.

a. Function0
b. Thing
c. Undefined
d. Undefined

22. _____ is a special mathematical relationship between two quantities. Two quantities are called proportional if they vary in such a way that one of the quantities is a constant multiple of the other, or equivalently if they have a constant ratio.
  a. Proportionality0
  b. Thing
  c. Undefined
  d. Undefined

23. In Euclidean geometry, a uniform _____ is a linear transformation that enlargers or diminishes objects, and whose _____ factor is the same in all directions. This is also called homothethy.
  a. Scale0
  b. Thing
  c. Undefined
  d. Undefined

24. _____ is a subset of a population.
  a. Sample0
  b. Thing
  c. Undefined
  d. Undefined

25. In elementary algebra, an _____ is a set that contains every real number between two indicated numbers and may contain the two numbers themselves.
  a. Thing
  b. Interval0
  c. Undefined
  d. Undefined

26. _____ is the middle point of a line segment.

## Chapter 8. Further Applications of Integration

  a. Thing
  b. Midpoint0
  c. Undefined
  d. Undefined

27. In geometry, a _____ is defined as a quadrilateral where all four of its angles are right angles.
  a. Thing
  b. Rectangle0
  c. Undefined
  d. Undefined

28. In mathematics, an _____, mean, or central tendency of a data set refers to a measure of the "middle" or "expected" value of the data set.
  a. Concept
  b. Average0
  c. Undefined
  d. Undefined

29. The _____, the average in everyday English, which is also called the arithmetic _____ (and is distinguished from the geometric _____ or harmonic _____). The average is also called the sample _____. The expected value of a random variable, which is also called the population _____.
  a. Mean0
  b. Thing
  c. Undefined
  d. Undefined

30. In probability theory and statistics, a _____ is a number dividing the higher half of a sample, a population, or a probability distribution from the lower half.
  a. Concept
  b. Median0
  c. Undefined
  d. Undefined

31. In mathematical analysis, _____ are objects which generalize functions and probability distributions.

## Chapter 8. Further Applications of Integration

  a. Distribution0
  b. Thing
  c. Undefined
  d. Undefined

32. In sociology and biology a _____ is the collection of people or organisms of a particular species living in a given geographic area or space, usually measured by a census.
  a. Thing
  b. Population0
  c. Undefined
  d. Undefined

33. _____ is a measure of difference for interval and ratio variables between the observed value and the mean.
  a. Deviation0
  b. Thing
  c. Undefined
  d. Undefined

34. _____ is a synonym for information.
  a. Data0
  b. Thing
  c. Undefined
  d. Undefined

35. _____ of a probability distribution, random variable, or population or multiset of values is a measure of the spread of its values.
  a. Standard deviation0
  b. Thing
  c. Undefined
  d. Undefined

36. A _____ given two distinct points A and B on the _____, is the set of points C on the line containing points A and B such that A is not strictly between C and B.

a. Thing
b. Ray0
c. Undefined
d. Undefined

*Chapter 9. Differential Equations* 61

1. _____ is a mathematical subject that includes the study of limits, derivatives, integrals, and power series and constitutes a major part of modern university curriculum.
    a. Calculus0
    b. Thing
    c. Undefined
    d. Undefined

2. In sociology and biology a _____ is the collection of people or organisms of a particular species living in a given geographic area or space, usually measured by a census.
    a. Population0
    b. Thing
    c. Undefined
    d. Undefined

3. In mathematics and the mathematical sciences, a _____ is a fixed, but possibly unspecified, value. This is in contrast to a variable, which is not fixed.
    a. Thing
    b. Constant0
    c. Undefined
    d. Undefined

4. A _____ of a number is the product of that number with any integer.
    a. Thing
    b. Multiple0
    c. Undefined
    d. Undefined

5. A _____ is a symbolic representation denoting a quantity or expression. It often represents an "unknown" quantity that has the potential to change.
    a. Thing
    b. Variable0
    c. Undefined
    d. Undefined

6. In mathematics, an _____ is any of the arguments, i.e. "inputs", to a function. Thus if we have a function f(x), then x is a _____.

## Chapter 9. Differential Equations

   a. Independent variable0
   b. Thing
   c. Undefined
   d. Undefined

7. _____ is often used to describe the measurement of the steepness, incline, gradient, or grade of a straight line. The _____ is defined as the ratio of the "rise" divided by the "run" between two points on a line, or in other words, the ratio of the altitude change to the horizontal distance between any two points on the line.
   a. Thing
   b. Slope0
   c. Undefined
   d. Undefined

8. A _____ is the result of the addition of a set of numbers. The numbers may be natural numbers, complex numbers, matrices, or still more complicated objects. An infinite _____ is a subtle procedure known as a series.
   a. Thing
   b. Sum0
   c. Undefined
   d. Undefined

9. In geometry, a line _____ is a part of a line that is bounded by two end points, and contains every point on the line between its end points.
   a. Segment0
   b. Concept
   c. Undefined
   d. Undefined

10. A _____ is a part of a line that is bounded by two end points, and contains every point on the line between its end points.
   a. Line segment0
   b. Thing
   c. Undefined
   d. Undefined

11. An _____ is a combination of numbers, operators, grouping symbols and/or free variables and bound variables arranged in a meaningful way which can be evaluated..

a. Expression0
b. Thing
c. Undefined
d. Undefined

12. An _____ is a straight line around which a geometric figure can be rotated.
   a. Thing
   b. Axis0
   c. Undefined
   d. Undefined

13. _____ means "constancy", i.e. if something retains a certain feature even after we change a way of looking at it, then it is symmetric.
   a. Thing
   b. Symmetry0
   c. Undefined
   d. Undefined

14. In botany, _____ are above-ground plant organs specialized for photosynthesis. Their characteristics are typically analyzed by using Fiobonacci's sequences.
   a. Leaves0
   b. Thing
   c. Undefined
   d. Undefined

15. In mathematics, a _____ is the result of multiplying, or an expression that identifies factors to be multiplied.
   a. Product0
   b. Thing
   c. Undefined
   d. Undefined

16. _____ is a branch of mathematics concerning the study of structure, relation and quantity.

a. Concept
b. Algebra0
c. Undefined
d. Undefined

17. _____ is a subset of a population.
a. Thing
b. Sample0
c. Undefined
d. Undefined

18. In elementary algebra, an _____ is a set that contains every real number between two indicated numbers and may contain the two numbers themselves.
a. Interval0
b. Thing
c. Undefined
d. Undefined

19. _____ is a synonym for information.
a. Thing
b. Data0
c. Undefined
d. Undefined

20. In mathematics, the _____ of a function is the set of all "output" values produced by that function. Given a function $f : A \to B$, the _____ of $f$, is defined to be the set $\{x \in B : x = f(a) \text{ for some } a \in A\}$.
a. Range0
b. Thing
c. Undefined
d. Undefined

21. A _____ is a numeral used to indicate a count. The most common use of the word today is to name the part of a fraction that tells the number or count of equal parts.

a. Numerator0
b. Thing
c. Undefined
d. Undefined


22. In classical geometry, a _____ of a circle or sphere is any line segment from its center to its boundary. By extension, the _____ of a circle or sphere is the length of any such segment. The _____ is half the diameter. In science and engineering the term _____ of curvature is commonly used as a synonym for _____.
a. Thing
b. Radius0
c. Undefined
d. Undefined


23. In mathematics, the _____ of a coordinate system is the point where the axes of the system intersect.
a. Thing
b. Origin0
c. Undefined
d. Undefined


24. _____ is mass m per unit volume V.
a. Thing
b. Density0
c. Undefined
d. Undefined

## Chapter 10. Parametric Equations and Polar Coordinates

1. A _____ is the quantity that defines certain relatively constant characteristics of systems or functions..
   a. Thing
   b. Parameter0
   c. Undefined
   d. Undefined

2. A _____ is a symbolic representation denoting a quantity or expression. It often represents an "unknown" quantity that has the potential to change.
   a. Variable0
   b. Thing
   c. Undefined
   d. Undefined

3. In Euclidean geometry, an _____ is a closed segment of a differentiable curve in the two-dimensional plane; for example, a circular _____ is a segment of a circle.
   a. Arc0
   b. Concept
   c. Undefined
   d. Undefined

4. In Euclidean geometry, a _____ is the set of all points in a plane at a fixed distance, called the radius, from a given point, the center.
   a. Thing
   b. Circle0
   c. Undefined
   d. Undefined

5. In elementary algebra, an _____ is a set that contains every real number between two indicated numbers and may contain the two numbers themselves.
   a. Thing
   b. Interval0
   c. Undefined
   d. Undefined

6. In geometry, a _____ is defined as a quadrilateral where all four of its angles are right angles.

## Chapter 10. Parametric Equations and Polar Coordinates

    a. Rectangle0
    b. Thing
    c. Undefined
    d. Undefined

7.   In mathematics, the additive inverse, or _____ of a number n is the number that, when added to n, yields zero. The additive inverse of n is denoted −n. For example, 7 is −7, because 7 + (−7) = 0, and the additive inverse of −0.3 is 0.3, because −0.3 + 0.3 = 0.
    a. Thing
    b. Opposite0
    c. Undefined
    d. Undefined

8.   In mathematics, the _____ of a number n is the number that, when added to n, yields zero. The _____ of n is denoted −n. For example, 7 is −7, because 7 + (−7) = 0, and the _____ of −0.3 is 0.3, because −0.3 + 0.3 = 0.
    a. Thing
    b. Additive inverse0
    c. Undefined
    d. Undefined

9.   In classical geometry, a _____ of a circle or sphere is any line segment from its center to its boundary. By extension, the _____ of a circle or sphere is the length of any such segment. The _____ is half the diameter. In science and engineering the term _____ of curvature is commonly used as a synonym for _____.
    a. Radius0
    b. Thing
    c. Undefined
    d. Undefined

10.   In the scientific method, an _____ (Latin: ex-+-periri, "of (or from) trying"), is a set of actions and observations, performed in the context of solving a particular problem or question, in order to support or falsify a hypothesis or research concerning phenomena.
    a. Thing
    b. Experiment0
    c. Undefined
    d. Undefined

## Chapter 10. Parametric Equations and Polar Coordinates

11. In mathematics, the _____ of a coordinate system is the point where the axes of the system intersect.
    a. Thing
    b. Origin0
    c. Undefined
    d. Undefined

12. An _____ is a collection of two not necessarily distinct objects, one of which is distinguished as the first coordinate and the other as the second coordinate.
    a. Thing
    b. Ordered pair0
    c. Undefined
    d. Undefined

13. In mathematics, a _____ is a two-dimensional manifold or surface that is perfectly flat.
    a. Plane0
    b. Thing
    c. Undefined
    d. Undefined

14. An _____ is a straight line around which a geometric figure can be rotated.
    a. Axis0
    b. Thing
    c. Undefined
    d. Undefined

15. A _____ is the part of the dividend that is left over when the dividend is not evenly divisible by the divisor.
    a. Thing
    b. Remainder0
    c. Undefined
    d. Undefined

16. _____ is often used to describe the measurement of the steepness, incline, gradient, or grade of a straight line. The _____ is defined as the ratio of the "rise" divided by the "run" between two points on a line, or in other words, the ratio of the altitude change to the horizontal distance between any two points on the line.

a. Slope0
b. Thing
c. Undefined
d. Undefined

17. In mathematics and the mathematical sciences, a _____ is a fixed, but possibly unspecified, value. This is in contrast to a variable, which is not fixed.
   a. Thing
   b. Constant0
   c. Undefined
   d. Undefined

18. A _____ is the result of the addition of a set of numbers. The numbers may be natural numbers, complex numbers, matrices, or still more complicated objects. An infinite _____ is a subtle procedure known as a series.
   a. Sum0
   b. Thing
   c. Undefined
   d. Undefined

19. In geometry, a line _____ is a part of a line that is bounded by two end points, and contains every point on the line between its end points.
   a. Concept
   b. Segment0
   c. Undefined
   d. Undefined

20. A _____ is a part of a line that is bounded by two end points, and contains every point on the line between its end points.
   a. Thing
   b. Line segment0
   c. Undefined
   d. Undefined

## Chapter 10. Parametric Equations and Polar Coordinates

21. In geometry, a _____ (Greek words diairo = divide and metro = measure) of a circle is any straight line segment that passes through the centre and whose endpoints are on the circular boundary, or, in more modern usage, the length of such a line segment. When using the word in the more modern sense, one speaks of the _____ rather than a _____, because all diameters of a circle have the same length. This length is twice the radius. The _____ of a circle is also the longest chord that the circle has.
    a. Diameter0
    b. Thing
    c. Undefined
    d. Undefined

22. _____ is a synonym for information.
    a. Thing
    b. Data0
    c. Undefined
    d. Undefined

23. The _____, the average in everyday English, which is also called the arithmetic _____ (and is distinguished from the geometric _____ or harmonic _____). The average is also called the sample _____. The expected value of a random variable, which is also called the population _____.
    a. Mean0
    b. Thing
    c. Undefined
    d. Undefined

24. _____ is a branch of mathematics concerning the study of structure, relation and quantity.
    a. Algebra0
    b. Concept
    c. Undefined
    d. Undefined

25. In plane geometry, a _____ is a polygon with four equal sides, four right angles, and parallel opposite sides. In algebra, the _____ of a number is that number multiplied by itself.
    a. Thing
    b. Square0
    c. Undefined
    d. Undefined

## Chapter 10. Parametric Equations and Polar Coordinates

26. A _____ is one of the basic shapes of geometry: a polygon with three vertices and three sides which are straight line segments.
   a. Triangle0
   b. Thing
   c. Undefined
   d. Undefined

27. In geometry, an _____ polygon is a polygon which has all sides of the same length.
   a. Equilateral0
   b. Thing
   c. Undefined
   d. Undefined

28. An _____ is a triangle in which all sides are of equal length.
   a. Equilateral triangle0
   b. Thing
   c. Undefined
   d. Undefined

## Chapter 11. Infinite Sequences and Series

1. In sociology and biology a _____ is the collection of people or organisms of a particular species living in a given geographic area or space, usually measured by a census.
   a. Thing
   b. Population0
   c. Undefined
   d. Undefined

2. In elementary algebra, an _____ is a set that contains every real number between two indicated numbers and may contain the two numbers themselves.
   a. Thing
   b. Interval0
   c. Undefined
   d. Undefined

3. A _____ is the part of a fraction that tells how many equal parts make up a whole, and which is used in the name of the fraction: "halves", "thirds", "fourths" or "quarters", "fifths" and so on.
   a. Denominator0
   b. Concept
   c. Undefined
   d. Undefined

4. An _____ is a combination of numbers, operators, grouping symbols and/or free variables and bound variables arranged in a meaningful way which can be evaluated..
   a. Expression0
   b. Thing
   c. Undefined
   d. Undefined

5. _____ or arithmetics is the oldest and most elementary branch of mathematics, used by almost everyone, for tasks ranging from simple daily counting to advanced science and business calculations.
   a. Thing
   b. Arithmetic0
   c. Undefined
   d. Undefined

## Chapter 11. Infinite Sequences and Series

6. The _____, the average in everyday English, which is also called the arithmetic _____ (and is distinguished from the geometric _____ or harmonic _____). The average is also called the sample _____. The expected value of a random variable, which is also called the population _____.
   a. Mean0
   b. Thing
   c. Undefined
   d. Undefined


7. A _____ is the result of the addition of a set of numbers. The numbers may be natural numbers, complex numbers, matrices, or still more complicated objects. An infinite _____ is a subtle procedure known as a series.
   a. Thing
   b. Sum0
   c. Undefined
   d. Undefined


8. In Euclidean geometry, a _____ is the set of all points in a plane at a fixed distance, called the radius, from a given point, the center.
   a. Circle0
   b. Thing
   c. Undefined
   d. Undefined


9. In classical geometry, a _____ of a circle or sphere is any line segment from its center to its boundary. By extension, the _____ of a circle or sphere is the length of any such segment. The _____ is half the diameter. In science and engineering the term _____ of curvature is commonly used as a synonym for _____.
   a. Radius0
   b. Thing
   c. Undefined
   d. Undefined


10. In plane geometry, a _____ is a polygon with four equal sides, four right angles, and parallel opposite sides. In algebra, the _____ of a number is that number multiplied by itself.
    a. Square0
    b. Thing
    c. Undefined
    d. Undefined

## Chapter 11. Infinite Sequences and Series

11. In the scientific method, an _____ (Latin: ex-+-periri, "of (or from) trying"), is a set of actions and observations, performed in the context of solving a particular problem or question, in order to support or falsify a hypothesis or research concerning phenomena.
    a. Experiment0
    b. Thing
    c. Undefined
    d. Undefined

12. A _____ is one of the basic shapes of geometry: a polygon with three vertices and three sides which are straight line segments.
    a. Thing
    b. Triangle0
    c. Undefined
    d. Undefined

13. In geometry, an _____ is a point at which a line segment or ray terminates.
    a. Thing
    b. Endpoint0
    c. Undefined
    d. Undefined

14. In geometry, a _____ is defined as a quadrilateral where all four of its angles are right angles.
    a. Rectangle0
    b. Thing
    c. Undefined
    d. Undefined

15. A _____ is the part of the dividend that is left over when the dividend is not evenly divisible by the divisor.
    a. Thing
    b. Remainder0
    c. Undefined
    d. Undefined

16. A _____ is a numeral used to indicate a count. The most common use of the word today is to name the part of a fraction that tells the number or count of equal parts.

a. Numerator0
b. Thing
c. Undefined
d. Undefined

17. In mathematics, the _____ (or modulus) of a real number is its numerical value without regard to its sign.
a. Absolute value0
b. Thing
c. Undefined
d. Undefined

18. A _____ is a quantity that denotes the proportional amount or magnitude of one quantity relative to another.
a. Ratio0
b. Thing
c. Undefined
d. Undefined

19. In mathematics, an inequality is a statement about the relative size or order of two objects. For example 14 > 10, or 14 is _____ 10.
a. Thing
b. Greater than0
c. Undefined
d. Undefined

20. _____ has many meanings, most of which simply .
a. Thing
b. Power0
c. Undefined
d. Undefined

21. _____ is a branch of mathematics concerning the study of structure, relation and quantity.

a. Concept
b. Algebra0
c. Undefined
d. Undefined

22. In mathematics, a _____ is an expression that is constructed from one or more variables and constants, using only the operations of addition, subtraction, multiplication, and constant positive whole number exponents. is a _____. Note in particular that division by an expression containing a variable is not in general allowed in polynomials. [1]
   a. Polynomial0
   b. Thing
   c. Undefined
   d. Undefined

23. In mathematics and the mathematical sciences, a _____ is a fixed, but possibly unspecified, value. This is in contrast to a variable, which is not fixed.
   a. Constant0
   b. Thing
   c. Undefined
   d. Undefined

24. In mathematics, the _____ of a coordinate system is the point where the axes of the system intersect.
   a. Origin0
   b. Thing
   c. Undefined
   d. Undefined

25. In elementary algebra, a _____ is a polynomial with two terms: the sum of two monomials. It is the simplest kind of polynomial except for a monomial.
   a. Thing
   b. Binomial0
   c. Undefined
   d. Undefined

26. An _____ is a straight line around which a geometric figure can be rotated.

## Chapter 11. Infinite Sequences and Series

a. Thing
b. Axis0
c. Undefined
d. Undefined

27. _____ is mass m per unit volume V.
a. Thing
b. Density0
c. Undefined
d. Undefined

28. In geometry, an _____ polygon is a polygon which has all sides of the same length.
a. Thing
b. Equilateral0
c. Undefined
d. Undefined

29. An _____ is a triangle in which all sides are of equal length.
a. Equilateral triangle0
b. Thing
c. Undefined
d. Undefined

30. In geometry a _____ is a plane figure that is bounded by a closed path or circuit, composed of a finite number of sequential line segments.
a. Thing
b. Polygon0
c. Undefined
d. Undefined

# Chapter 12. Vectors and the Geometry of Space

1. In mathematics, a _____ is a two-dimensional manifold or surface that is perfectly flat.
   a. Plane0
   b. Thing
   c. Undefined
   d. Undefined

2. In mathematics, the _____ of a coordinate system is the point where the axes of the system intersect.
   a. Thing
   b. Origin0
   c. Undefined
   d. Undefined

3. In classical geometry, a _____ of a circle or sphere is any line segment from its center to its boundary. By extension, the _____ of a circle or sphere is the length of any such segment. The _____ is half the diameter. In science and engineering the term _____ of curvature is commonly used as a synonym for _____.
   a. Thing
   b. Radius0
   c. Undefined
   d. Undefined

4. In mathematics, the additive inverse, or _____ of a number n is the number that, when added to n, yields zero. The additive inverse of n is denoted −n. For example, 7 is −7, because 7 + (−7) = 0, and the additive inverse of −0.3 is 0.3, because −0.3 + 0.3 = 0.
   a. Thing
   b. Opposite0
   c. Undefined
   d. Undefined

5. In mathematics, the _____ of a number n is the number that, when added to n, yields zero. The _____ of n is denoted −n. For example, 7 is −7, because 7 + (−7) = 0, and the _____ of −0.3 is 0.3, because −0.3 + 0.3 = 0.
   a. Thing
   b. Additive inverse0
   c. Undefined
   d. Undefined

6. In geometry, a line _____ is a part of a line that is bounded by two end points, and contains every point on the line between its end points.

a. Concept
b. Segment0
c. Undefined
d. Undefined

7. A _____ is a part of a line that is bounded by two end points, and contains every point on the line between its end points.
   a. Line segment0
   b. Thing
   c. Undefined
   d. Undefined

8. An _____ is a collection of two not necessarily distinct objects, one of which is distinguished as the first coordinate and the other as the second coordinate.
   a. Ordered pair0
   b. Thing
   c. Undefined
   d. Undefined

9. In mathematics, a _____ may be described informally as a number that can be given by an infinite decimal representation.
   a. Thing
   b. Real number0
   c. Undefined
   d. Undefined

10. In mathematics, a _____ is an n-tuple with n being 3.
    a. Thing
    b. Triple0
    c. Undefined
    d. Undefined

11. In mathematics, _____ is an elementary arithmetic operation. When one of the numbers is a whole number, _____ is the repeated sum of the other number.

a. Multiplication0
b. Thing
c. Undefined
d. Undefined

12. A _____ is the result of the addition of a set of numbers. The numbers may be natural numbers, complex numbers, matrices, or still more complicated objects. An infinite _____ is a subtle procedure known as a series.
   a. Sum0
   b. Thing
   c. Undefined
   d. Undefined

13. A _____ is a four-sided plane figure that has two sets of opposite parallel sides.
   a. Concept
   b. Parallelogram0
   c. Undefined
   d. Undefined

14. In sociology and biology a _____ is the collection of people or organisms of a particular species living in a given geographic area or space, usually measured by a census.
   a. Thing
   b. Population0
   c. Undefined
   d. Undefined

15. _____ is the middle point of a line segment.
   a. Thing
   b. Midpoint0
   c. Undefined
   d. Undefined

16. A _____ given two distinct points A and B on the _____, is the set of points C on the line containing points A and B such that A is not strictly between C and B.

a. Thing
b. Ray0
c. Undefined
d. Undefined


17. In mathematics, a _____ is the result of multiplying, or an expression that identifies factors to be multiplied.
a. Product0
b. Thing
c. Undefined
d. Undefined


18. An _____ is a combination of numbers, operators, grouping symbols and/or free variables and bound variables arranged in a meaningful way which can be evaluated..
a. Expression0
b. Thing
c. Undefined
d. Undefined


19. A _____ is one of the basic shapes of geometry: a polygon with three vertices and three sides which are straight line segments.
a. Thing
b. Triangle0
c. Undefined
d. Undefined


20. An _____ is a straight line around which a geometric figure can be rotated.
a. Thing
b. Axis0
c. Undefined
d. Undefined


21. In mathematics, the multiplicative inverse of a number x, denoted 1/x or $x^{-1}$, is the number which, when multiplied by x, yields 1. The multiplicative inverse of x is also called the _____ of x.

## Chapter 12. Vectors and the Geometry of Space

  a. Thing
  b. Reciprocal0
  c. Undefined
  d. Undefined

22. A _____ is a symbolic representation denoting a quantity or expression. It often represents an "unknown" quantity that has the potential to change.
  a. Thing
  b. Variable0
  c. Undefined
  d. Undefined

23. In Euclidean geometry, a _____ is the set of all points in a plane at a fixed distance, called the radius, from a given point, the center.
  a. Thing
  b. Circle0
  c. Undefined
  d. Undefined

24. In mathematics and the mathematical sciences, a _____ is a fixed, but possibly unspecified, value. This is in contrast to a variable, which is not fixed.
  a. Constant0
  b. Thing
  c. Undefined
  d. Undefined

25. _____ has many meanings, most of which simply .
  a. Thing
  b. Power0
  c. Undefined
  d. Undefined

26. _____ means "constancy", i.e. if something retains a certain feature even after we change a way of looking at it, then it is symmetric.

## Chapter 12. Vectors and the Geometry of Space

a. Symmetry0
b. Thing
c. Undefined
d. Undefined

27. In the scientific method, an _____ (Latin: ex-+-periri, "of (or from) trying"), is a set of actions and observations, performed in the context of solving a particular problem or question, in order to support or falsify a hypothesis or research concerning phenomena.
  a. Experiment0
  b. Thing
  c. Undefined
  d. Undefined

28. In mathematics, a _____ number (or a _____) is a natural number that has exactly two (distinct) natural number divisors, which are 1 and the _____ number itself.
  a. Prime0
  b. Thing
  c. Undefined
  d. Undefined

29. The _____ are the only integral domain whose positive elements are well-ordered, and in which order is preserved by addition. Like the natural numbers, the _____ form a countably infinite set. The set of all _____ is usually denoted in mathematics by a boldface Z .
  a. Integers0
  b. Thing
  c. Undefined
  d. Undefined

1. In mathematics, the _____ of a function is the set of all "output" values produced by that function. Given a function $f : A \to B$, the _____ of $f$, is defined to be the set $\{x \in B : x = f(a) \text{ for some } a \in A\}$.
   a. Thing
   b. Range0
   c. Undefined
   d. Undefined

2. In mathematics, a _____ may be described informally as a number that can be given by an infinite decimal representation.
   a. Real number0
   b. Thing
   c. Undefined
   d. Undefined

3. An _____ is a combination of numbers, operators, grouping symbols and/or free variables and bound variables arranged in a meaningful way which can be evaluated..
   a. Expression0
   b. Thing
   c. Undefined
   d. Undefined

4. In elementary algebra, an _____ is a set that contains every real number between two indicated numbers and may contain the two numbers themselves.
   a. Thing
   b. Interval0
   c. Undefined
   d. Undefined

5. A _____ is the quantity that defines certain relatively constant characteristics of systems or functions..
   a. Parameter0
   b. Thing
   c. Undefined
   d. Undefined

6. In mathematics, a _____ is a two-dimensional manifold or surface that is perfectly flat.

a. Thing
b. Plane0
c. Undefined
d. Undefined


7. A _____ of a number is the product of that number with any integer.
a. Multiple0
b. Thing
c. Undefined
d. Undefined


8. In mathematics, a _____ is the result of multiplying, or an expression that identifies factors to be multiplied.
a. Product0
b. Thing
c. Undefined
d. Undefined


9. In mathematics and the mathematical sciences, a _____ is a fixed, but possibly unspecified, value. This is in contrast to a variable, which is not fixed.
a. Thing
b. Constant0
c. Undefined
d. Undefined


10. In Euclidean geometry, an _____ is a closed segment of a differentiable curve in the two-dimensional plane; for example, a circular _____ is a segment of a circle.
a. Concept
b. Arc0
c. Undefined
d. Undefined


11. In elementary algebra, a _____ is a polynomial with two terms: the sum of two monomials. It is the simplest kind of polynomial except for a monomial.

a. Thing
b. Binomial0
c. Undefined
d. Undefined

12. In mathematics, an _____, mean, or central tendency of a data set refers to a measure of the "middle" or "expected" value of the data set.
a. Concept
b. Average0
c. Undefined
d. Undefined

13. In mathematics, the additive inverse, or _____ of a number n is the number that, when added to n, yields zero. The additive inverse of n is denoted −n. For example, 7 is −7, because 7 + (−7) = 0, and the additive inverse of −0.3 is 0.3, because −0.3 + 0.3 = 0.
a. Thing
b. Opposite0
c. Undefined
d. Undefined

14. In mathematics, the _____ of a number n is the number that, when added to n, yields zero. The _____ of n is denoted −n. For example, 7 is −7, because 7 + (−7) = 0, and the _____ of −0.3 is 0.3, because −0.3 + 0.3 = 0.
a. Thing
b. Additive inverse0
c. Undefined
d. Undefined

15. In mathematics, the _____ of a coordinate system is the point where the axes of the system intersect.
a. Origin0
b. Thing
c. Undefined
d. Undefined

16. In classical geometry, a _____ of a circle or sphere is any line segment from its center to its boundary. By extension, the _____ of a circle or sphere is the length of any such segment. The _____ is half the diameter. In science and engineering the term _____ of curvature is commonly used as a synonym for _____.

a. Radius0
b. Thing
c. Undefined
d. Undefined

17. _____ is a synonym for information.
a. Data0
b. Thing
c. Undefined
d. Undefined

18. An _____ is a straight line around which a geometric figure can be rotated.
a. Thing
b. Axis0
c. Undefined
d. Undefined

19. In Euclidean geometry, a _____ is the set of all points in a plane at a fixed distance, called the radius, from a given point, the center.
a. Thing
b. Circle0
c. Undefined
d. Undefined

20. _____ is often used to describe the measurement of the steepness, incline, gradient, or grade of a straight line. The _____ is defined as the ratio of the "rise" divided by the "run" between two points on a line, or in other words, the ratio of the altitude change to the horizontal distance between any two points on the line.
a. Slope0
b. Thing
c. Undefined
d. Undefined

# Chapter 14. Partial Derivatives

1. An _____ is a collection of two not necessarily distinct objects, one of which is distinguished as the first coordinate and the other as the second coordinate.
   a. Ordered pair0
   b. Thing
   c. Undefined
   d. Undefined

2. In mathematics, the _____ of a function is the set of all "output" values produced by that function. Given a function $f : A \to B$, the _____ of $f$, is defined to be the set $\{x \in B : x = f(a) \text{ for some } a \in A\}$.
   a. Range0
   b. Thing
   c. Undefined
   d. Undefined

3. In mathematics, a _____ may be described informally as a number that can be given by an infinite decimal representation.
   a. Thing
   b. Real number0
   c. Undefined
   d. Undefined

4. A _____ is a symbolic representation denoting a quantity or expression. It often represents an "unknown" quantity that has the potential to change.
   a. Variable0
   b. Thing
   c. Undefined
   d. Undefined

5. An _____ is a combination of numbers, operators, grouping symbols and/or free variables and bound variables arranged in a meaningful way which can be evaluated..
   a. Expression0
   b. Thing
   c. Undefined
   d. Undefined

6. In mathematics, factorization (British English: factorisation) or factoring is the decomposition of an object (for example, a number, a polynomial, or a matrix) into a product of other objects, or _____, which when multiplied together give the original.
   a. Thing
   b. Factors0
   c. Undefined
   d. Undefined

7. In mathematics, a _____ is a two-dimensional manifold or surface that is perfectly flat.
   a. Thing
   b. Plane0
   c. Undefined
   d. Undefined

8. The word _____ comes from the Latin word linearis, which means created by lines.
   a. Thing
   b. Linear0
   c. Undefined
   d. Undefined

9. A _____ is a first degree polynomial mathematical function of the form: f(x) = mx + b where m and b are real constants and x is a real variable.
   a. Linear function0
   b. Thing
   c. Undefined
   d. Undefined

10. The mathematical concept of a _____ expresses the intuitive idea of deterministic dependence between two quantities, one of which is viewed as primary and the other as secondary. A _____ then is a way to associate a unique output for each input of a specified type, for example, a real number or an element of a given set.
    a. Thing
    b. Function0
    c. Undefined
    d. Undefined

## Chapter 14. Partial Derivatives

11. In mathematics and the mathematical sciences, a _____ is a fixed, but possibly unspecified, value. This is in contrast to a variable, which is not fixed.
    a. Thing
    b. Constant0
    c. Undefined
    d. Undefined

12. The existence and properties of _____ are the basis of Euclid's parallel postulate. _____ are two lines on the same plane that do not intersect even assuming that lines extend to infinity in either direction.
    a. Parallel lines0
    b. Thing
    c. Undefined
    d. Undefined

13. In classical geometry, a _____ of a circle or sphere is any line segment from its center to its boundary. By extension, the _____ of a circle or sphere is the length of any such segment. The _____ is half the diameter. In science and engineering the term _____ of curvature is commonly used as a synonym for _____.
    a. Radius0
    b. Thing
    c. Undefined
    d. Undefined

14. In mathematics, the _____ of a coordinate system is the point where the axes of the system intersect.
    a. Origin0
    b. Thing
    c. Undefined
    d. Undefined

15. The _____ are the only integral domain whose positive elements are well-ordered, and in which order is preserved by addition. Like the natural numbers, the _____ form a countably infinite set. The set of all _____ is usually denoted in mathematics by a boldface Z .
    a. Integers0
    b. Thing
    c. Undefined
    d. Undefined

## Chapter 14. Partial Derivatives

16. In mathematics, a _____ is an expression that is constructed from one or more variables and constants, using only the operations of addition, subtraction, multiplication, and constant positive whole number exponents. is a _____. Note in particular that division by an expression containing a variable is not in general allowed in polynomials. [1]
    a. Polynomial0
    b. Thing
    c. Undefined
    d. Undefined

17. A _____ is the result of the addition of a set of numbers. The numbers may be natural numbers, complex numbers, matrices, or still more complicated objects. An infinite _____ is a subtle procedure known as a series.
    a. Sum0
    b. Thing
    c. Undefined
    d. Undefined

18. In mathematics, _____ is an elementary arithmetic operation. When one of the numbers is a whole number, _____ is the repeated sum of the other number.
    a. Thing
    b. Multiplication0
    c. Undefined
    d. Undefined

19. In mathematics, a _____ is the end result of a division problem. It can also be expressed as the number of times the divisor divides into the dividend.
    a. Quotient0
    b. Thing
    c. Undefined
    d. Undefined

20. In mathematics, a _____ is the result of multiplying, or an expression that identifies factors to be multiplied.
    a. Thing
    b. Product0
    c. Undefined
    d. Undefined

## Chapter 14. Partial Derivatives

21. _____ is often used to describe the measurement of the steepness, incline, gradient, or grade of a straight line. The _____ is defined as the ratio of the "rise" divided by the "run" between two points on a line, or in other words, the ratio of the altitude change to the horizontal distance between any two points on the line.
   a. Slope0
   b. Thing
   c. Undefined
   d. Undefined

22. _____ is a branch of mathematics concerning the study of structure, relation and quantity.
   a. Algebra0
   b. Concept
   c. Undefined
   d. Undefined

23. _____ is mass m per unit volume V.
   a. Density0
   b. Thing
   c. Undefined
   d. Undefined

24. In mathematics, the additive inverse, or _____ of a number n is the number that, when added to n, yields zero. The additive inverse of n is denoted −n. For example, 7 is −7, because 7 + (−7) = 0, and the additive inverse of −0.3 is 0.3, because −0.3 + 0.3 = 0.
   a. Thing
   b. Opposite0
   c. Undefined
   d. Undefined

25. In mathematics, the _____ of a number n is the number that, when added to n, yields zero. The _____ of n is denoted −n. For example, 7 is −7, because 7 + (−7) = 0, and the _____ of −0.3 is 0.3, because −0.3 + 0.3 = 0.
   a. Additive inverse0
   b. Thing
   c. Undefined
   d. Undefined

## Chapter 14. Partial Derivatives

26. A _____ is one of the basic shapes of geometry: a polygon with three vertices and three sides which are straight line segments.
   a. Thing
   b. Triangle0
   c. Undefined
   d. Undefined

27. _____ is the estimation of a physical quantity such as distance, energy, temperature, or time.
   a. Thing
   b. Measurement0
   c. Undefined
   d. Undefined

28. In mathematics, an _____ is any of the arguments, i.e. "inputs", to a function. Thus if we have a function f(x), then x is a _____.
   a. Thing
   b. Independent variable0
   c. Undefined
   d. Undefined

29. In geometry, a _____ is defined as a quadrilateral where all four of its angles are right angles.
   a. Thing
   b. Rectangle0
   c. Undefined
   d. Undefined

30. In plane geometry, a _____ is a polygon with four equal sides, four right angles, and parallel opposite sides. In algebra, the _____ of a number is that number multiplied by itself.
   a. Square0
   b. Thing
   c. Undefined
   d. Undefined

31. _____ is a mathematical subject that includes the study of limits, derivatives, integrals, and power series and constitutes a major part of modern university curriculum.

a. Thing
b. Calculus0
c. Undefined
d. Undefined

32. In elementary algebra, an _____ is a set that contains every real number between two indicated numbers and may contain the two numbers themselves.
   a. Thing
   b. Interval0
   c. Undefined
   d. Undefined

33. In Euclidean geometry, a _____ is the set of all points in a plane at a fixed distance, called the radius, from a given point, the center.
   a. Thing
   b. Circle0
   c. Undefined
   d. Undefined

34. _____ is a synonym for information.
   a. Thing
   b. Data0
   c. Undefined
   d. Undefined

35. In the scientific method, an _____ (Latin: ex-+-periri, "of (or from) trying"), is a set of actions and observations, performed in the context of solving a particular problem or question, in order to support or falsify a hypothesis or research concerning phenomena.
   a. Thing
   b. Experiment0
   c. Undefined
   d. Undefined

36. _____ is a measure of difference for interval and ratio variables between the observed value and the mean.

## Chapter 14. Partial Derivatives

a. Deviation0
b. Thing
c. Undefined
d. Undefined

37. In regression analysis, _____, also known as ordinary _____ analysis is a method for linear regression that determines the values of unknown quantities in a statistical model by minimizing the sum of the residuals difference between the predicted and observed values squared.

a. Thing
b. Least squares0
c. Undefined
d. Undefined

38. _____ or arithmetics is the oldest and most elementary branch of mathematics, used by almost everyone, for tasks ranging from simple daily counting to advanced science and business calculations.

a. Arithmetic0
b. Thing
c. Undefined
d. Undefined

39. The _____, the average in everyday English, which is also called the arithmetic _____ (and is distinguished from the geometric _____ or harmonic _____). The average is also called the sample _____. The expected value of a random variable, which is also called the population _____.

a. Thing
b. Mean0
c. Undefined
d. Undefined

## Chapter 15. Multiple Integrals

1. A _____ is a symbolic representation denoting a quantity or expression. It often represents an "unknown" quantity that has the potential to change.
   a. Variable0
   b. Thing
   c. Undefined
   d. Undefined

2. In geometry, a _____ is defined as a quadrilateral where all four of its angles are right angles.
   a. Thing
   b. Rectangle0
   c. Undefined
   d. Undefined

3. A _____ is the result of the addition of a set of numbers. The numbers may be natural numbers, complex numbers, matrices, or still more complicated objects. An infinite _____ is a subtle procedure known as a series.
   a. Sum0
   b. Thing
   c. Undefined
   d. Undefined

4. In classical geometry, a _____ of a circle or sphere is any line segment from its center to its boundary. By extension, the _____ of a circle or sphere is the length of any such segment. The _____ is half the diameter. In science and engineering the term _____ of curvature is commonly used as a synonym for _____.
   a. Radius0
   b. Thing
   c. Undefined
   d. Undefined

5. In mathematics, an _____, mean, or central tendency of a data set refers to a measure of the "middle" or "expected" value of the data set.
   a. Concept
   b. Average0
   c. Undefined
   d. Undefined

6. In mathematics and the mathematical sciences, a _____ is a fixed, but possibly unspecified, value. This is in contrast to a variable, which is not fixed.

## Chapter 15. Multiple Integrals

a. Thing
b. Constant0
c. Undefined
d. Undefined

7. _____ is a subset of a population.
   a. Thing
   b. Sample0
   c. Undefined
   d. Undefined

8. _____ is the middle point of a line segment.
   a. Thing
   b. Midpoint0
   c. Undefined
   d. Undefined

9. In mathematics, the _____ of a coordinate system is the point where the axes of the system intersect.
   a. Origin0
   b. Thing
   c. Undefined
   d. Undefined

10. In plane geometry, a _____ is a polygon with four equal sides, four right angles, and parallel opposite sides. In algebra, the _____ of a number is that number multiplied by itself.
    a. Square0
    b. Thing
    c. Undefined
    d. Undefined

11. In mathematics, a _____ is a two-dimensional manifold or surface that is perfectly flat.

a. Thing
b. Plane0
c. Undefined
d. Undefined

12. In Euclidean geometry, a _____ is the set of all points in a plane at a fixed distance, called the radius, from a given point, the center.
   a. Circle0
   b. Thing
   c. Undefined
   d. Undefined

13. An _____ is a combination of numbers, operators, grouping symbols and/or free variables and bound variables arranged in a meaningful way which can be evaluated..
   a. Expression0
   b. Thing
   c. Undefined
   d. Undefined

14. _____ is mass m per unit volume V.
   a. Density0
   b. Thing
   c. Undefined
   d. Undefined

15. A _____ is one of the basic shapes of geometry: a polygon with three vertices and three sides which are straight line segments.
   a. Thing
   b. Triangle0
   c. Undefined
   d. Undefined

16. An _____ is a straight line around which a geometric figure can be rotated.

## Chapter 15. Multiple Integrals

a. Axis0
b. Thing
c. Undefined
d. Undefined

17. _____ is the chance that something is likely to happen or be the case.
a. Probability0
b. Thing
c. Undefined
d. Undefined

18. _____ is a measure of difference for interval and ratio variables between the observed value and the mean.
a. Thing
b. Deviation0
c. Undefined
d. Undefined

19. The _____, the average in everyday English, which is also called the arithmetic _____ (and is distinguished from the geometric _____ or harmonic _____). The average is also called the sample _____. The expected value of a random variable, which is also called the population _____.
a. Mean0
b. Thing
c. Undefined
d. Undefined

20. _____ is a function that represents a probability distribution in terms of integrals.
a. Thing
b. Probability density function0
c. Undefined
d. Undefined

21. The mathematical concept of a _____ expresses the intuitive idea of deterministic dependence between two quantities, one of which is viewed as primary and the other as secondary. A _____ then is a way to associate a unique output for each input of a specified type, for example, a real number or an element of a given set.

a. Function0
b. Thing
c. Undefined
d. Undefined

22. _____ is a quantity whose values are random and to which a probability distribution is assigned.
a. Thing
b. Random variable0
c. Undefined
d. Undefined

23. In geometry, a _____ (Greek words diairo = divide and metro = measure) of a circle is any straight line segment that passes through the centre and whose endpoints are on the circular boundary, or, in more modern usage, the length of such a line segment. When using the word in the more modern sense, one speaks of the _____ rather than a _____, because all diameters of a circle have the same length. This length is twice the radius. The _____ of a circle is also the longest chord that the circle has.
a. Diameter0
b. Thing
c. Undefined
d. Undefined

24. _____ is a branch of mathematics concerning the study of structure, relation and quantity.
a. Algebra0
b. Concept
c. Undefined
d. Undefined

25. In mathematics, a _____ is an n-tuple with n being 3.
a. Thing
b. Triple0
c. Undefined
d. Undefined

26. A _____ of a number is the product of that number with any integer.

a. Multiple0
b. Thing
c. Undefined
d. Undefined

27. In mathematics, the _____ of a function is the set of all "output" values produced by that function. Given a function $f : A \to B$, the _____ of $f$, is defined to be the set $\{x \in B : x = f(a) \text{ for some } a \in A\}$.
   a. Range0
   b. Thing
   c. Undefined
   d. Undefined

28. A _____ is a four-sided plane figure that has two sets of opposite parallel sides.
   a. Concept
   b. Parallelogram0
   c. Undefined
   d. Undefined

29. _____ is a mathematical subject that includes the study of limits, derivatives, integrals, and power series and constitutes a major part of modern university curriculum.
   a. Thing
   b. Calculus0
   c. Undefined
   d. Undefined

## Chapter 16. Vector Calculus

1. In Euclidean geometry, a _____ is the set of all points in a plane at a fixed distance, called the radius, from a given point, the center.
   a. Thing
   b. Circle0
   c. Undefined
   d. Undefined

2. In classical geometry, a _____ of a circle or sphere is any line segment from its center to its boundary. By extension, the _____ of a circle or sphere is the length of any such segment. The _____ is half the diameter. In science and engineering the term _____ of curvature is commonly used as a synonym for _____.
   a. Radius0
   b. Thing
   c. Undefined
   d. Undefined

3. In mathematics, the _____ of a coordinate system is the point where the axes of the system intersect.
   a. Origin0
   b. Thing
   c. Undefined
   d. Undefined

4. A _____ is the quantity that defines certain relatively constant characteristics of systems or functions..
   a. Parameter0
   b. Thing
   c. Undefined
   d. Undefined

5. In geometry, a line _____ is a part of a line that is bounded by two end points, and contains every point on the line between its end points.
   a. Concept
   b. Segment0
   c. Undefined
   d. Undefined

6. A _____ is a part of a line that is bounded by two end points, and contains every point on the line between its end points.

a. Line segment0
b. Thing
c. Undefined
d. Undefined

7. _____ is a branch of mathematics concerning the study of structure, relation and quantity.
   a. Concept
   b. Algebra0
   c. Undefined
   d. Undefined

8. In mathematics and the mathematical sciences, a _____ is a fixed, but possibly unspecified, value. This is in contrast to a variable, which is not fixed.
   a. Constant0
   b. Thing
   c. Undefined
   d. Undefined

9. _____ is mass m per unit volume V.
   a. Thing
   b. Density0
   c. Undefined
   d. Undefined

10. _____ is a mathematical subject that includes the study of limits, derivatives, integrals, and power series and constitutes a major part of modern university curriculum.
    a. Calculus0
    b. Thing
    c. Undefined
    d. Undefined

11. In mathematics, a _____ is a two-dimensional manifold or surface that is perfectly flat.

## Chapter 16. Vector Calculus

   a. Plane0
   b. Thing
   c. Undefined
   d. Undefined

12. In mathematics, the additive inverse, or _____ of a number n is the number that, when added to n, yields zero. The additive inverse of n is denoted −n. For example, 7 is −7, because 7 + (−7) = 0, and the additive inverse of −0.3 is 0.3, because −0.3 + 0.3 = 0.
   a. Opposite0
   b. Thing
   c. Undefined
   d. Undefined

13. In mathematics, the _____ of a number n is the number that, when added to n, yields zero. The _____ of n is denoted −n. For example, 7 is −7, because 7 + (−7) = 0, and the _____ of −0.3 is 0.3, because −0.3 + 0.3 = 0.
   a. Thing
   b. Additive inverse0
   c. Undefined
   d. Undefined

14. In plane geometry, a _____ is a polygon with four equal sides, four right angles, and parallel opposite sides. In algebra, the _____ of a number is that number multiplied by itself.
   a. Square0
   b. Thing
   c. Undefined
   d. Undefined

15. In elementary algebra, an _____ is a set that contains every real number between two indicated numbers and may contain the two numbers themselves.
   a. Interval0
   b. Thing
   c. Undefined
   d. Undefined

16. A _____ is one of the basic shapes of geometry: a polygon with three vertices and three sides which are straight line segments.

a. Thing
b. Triangle0
c. Undefined
d. Undefined

17. In geometry, a _____ is any five-sided polygon.
a. Thing
b. Pentagon0
c. Undefined
d. Undefined

18. In geometry a _____ is a plane figure that is bounded by a closed path or circuit, composed of a finite number of sequential line segments.
a. Thing
b. Polygon0
c. Undefined
d. Undefined

19. An _____ is a straight line around which a geometric figure can be rotated.
a. Thing
b. Axis0
c. Undefined
d. Undefined

20. A _____ is a symbolic representation denoting a quantity or expression. It often represents an "unknown" quantity that has the potential to change.
a. Variable0
b. Thing
c. Undefined
d. Undefined

21. In mathematics, a _____ may be described informally as a number that can be given by an infinite decimal representation.

a. Thing
b. Real number0
c. Undefined
d. Undefined

22. A _____ is a four-sided plane figure that has two sets of opposite parallel sides.
a. Concept
b. Parallelogram0
c. Undefined
d. Undefined

## Chapter 17. Second-Order Differential Equations

1. In mathematics and the mathematical sciences, a _____ is a fixed, but possibly unspecified, value. This is in contrast to a variable, which is not fixed.
   a. Thing
   b. Constant0
   c. Undefined
   d. Undefined

2. A _____ of a number is the product of that number with any integer.
   a. Multiple0
   b. Thing
   c. Undefined
   d. Undefined

3. In elementary algebra, an _____ is a set that contains every real number between two indicated numbers and may contain the two numbers themselves.
   a. Thing
   b. Interval0
   c. Undefined
   d. Undefined

4. In mathematics, a _____ is an expression that is constructed from one or more variables and constants, using only the operations of addition, subtraction, multiplication, and constant positive whole number exponents. is a _____. Note in particular that division by an expression containing a variable is not in general allowed in polynomials. [1]
   a. Polynomial0
   b. Thing
   c. Undefined
   d. Undefined

5. In mathematics, a _____ is a two-dimensional manifold or surface that is perfectly flat.
   a. Thing
   b. Plane0
   c. Undefined
   d. Undefined

6. A _____ is the quantity that defines certain relatively constant characteristics of systems or functions..

a. Parameter0
b. Thing
c. Undefined
d. Undefined

7. _____ is a branch of mathematics concerning the study of structure, relation and quantity.
a. Algebra0
b. Concept
c. Undefined
d. Undefined

8. _____ is a mathematical subject that includes the study of limits, derivatives, integrals, and power series and constitutes a major part of modern university curriculum.
a. Thing
b. Calculus0
c. Undefined
d. Undefined

9. In geometry, a _____ is defined as a quadrilateral where all four of its angles are right angles.
a. Rectangle0
b. Thing
c. Undefined
d. Undefined

10. In mathematics, the additive inverse, or _____ of a number n is the number that, when added to n, yields zero. The additive inverse of n is denoted −n. For example, 7 is −7, because 7 + (−7) = 0, and the additive inverse of −0.3 is 0.3, because −0.3 + 0.3 = 0.
a. Thing
b. Opposite0
c. Undefined
d. Undefined

11. In mathematics, the _____ of a number n is the number that, when added to n, yields zero. The _____ of n is denoted −n. For example, 7 is −7, because 7 + (−7) = 0, and the _____ of −0.3 is 0.3, because −0.3 + 0.3 = 0.

## Chapter 17. Second-Order Differential Equations

a. Additive inverse0
b. Thing
c. Undefined
d. Undefined


12. In plane geometry, a _____ is a polygon with four equal sides, four right angles, and parallel opposite sides. In algebra, the _____ of a number is that number multiplied by itself.
   a. Square0
   b. Thing
   c. Undefined
   d. Undefined


13. _____ is mass m per unit volume V.
   a. Thing
   b. Density0
   c. Undefined
   d. Undefined


14. An _____ is a straight line around which a geometric figure can be rotated.
   a. Axis0
   b. Thing
   c. Undefined
   d. Undefined


15. In classical geometry, a _____ of a circle or sphere is any line segment from its center to its boundary. By extension, the _____ of a circle or sphere is the length of any such segment. The _____ is half the diameter. In science and engineering the term _____ of curvature is commonly used as a synonym for _____.
   a. Radius0
   b. Thing
   c. Undefined
   d. Undefined


16. In mathematics, a _____ is an n-tuple with n being 3.

a. Triple0
b. Thing
c. Undefined
d. Undefined

17. An _____ is a combination of numbers, operators, grouping symbols and/or free variables and bound variables arranged in a meaningful way which can be evaluated..
    a. Expression0
    b. Thing
    c. Undefined
    d. Undefined

18. _____ has many meanings, most of which simply .
    a. Thing
    b. Power0
    c. Undefined
    d. Undefined

19. The word _____ comes from the Latin word linearis, which means created by lines.
    a. Linear0
    b. Thing
    c. Undefined
    d. Undefined

20. A _____ is an equation in which each term is either a constant or the product of a constant times the first power of a variable.
    a. Linear equation0
    b. Thing
    c. Undefined
    d. Undefined

21. A _____ is the result of the addition of a set of numbers. The numbers may be natural numbers, complex numbers, matrices, or still more complicated objects. An infinite _____ is a subtle procedure known as a series.

a. Sum0
b. Thing
c. Undefined
d. Undefined


22. In statistics the _____ of an event i is the number $n_i$ of times the event occurred in the experiment or the study. These frequencies are often graphically represented in histograms.
    a. Concept
    b. Frequency0
    c. Undefined
    d. Undefined

## Chapter 1

| | | | | | | | | | |
|---|---|---|---|---|---|---|---|---|---|
| 1. a | 2. a | 3. a | 4. b | 5. b | 6. b | 7. a | 8. a | 9. a | 10. a |
| 11. a | 12. a | 13. a | 14. b | 15. a | 16. b | 17. b | 18. a | 19. b | 20. b |
| 21. a | 22. a | 23. b | 24. b | 25. a | 26. b | 27. b | 28. a | 29. b | 30. a |
| 31. b | 32. a | 33. b | 34. a | 35. b | 36. a | 37. b | 38. b | 39. b | 40. a |
| 41. a | 42. a | 43. b | | | | | | | |

## Chapter 2

| | | | | | | | | | |
|---|---|---|---|---|---|---|---|---|---|
| 1. a | 2. b | 3. b | 4. a | 5. a | 6. b | 7. b | 8. a | 9. b | 10. b |
| 11. b | 12. a | 13. a | 14. a | 15. a | 16. b | 17. b | 18. a | 19. b | 20. b |
| 21. a | 22. b | 23. b | 24. b | 25. a | 26. a | | | | |

## Chapter 3

| | | | | | | | | | |
|---|---|---|---|---|---|---|---|---|---|
| 1. b | 2. a | 3. a | 4. a | 5. a | 6. b | 7. b | 8. a | 9. a | 10. a |
| 11. b | 12. a | 13. a | 14. b | 15. b | 16. a | 17. b | 18. b | 19. a | 20. b |
| 21. a | 22. a | 23. b | 24. b | 25. b | 26. b | 27. b | 28. a | 29. b | 30. b |
| 31. a | 32. a | 33. b | 34. a | 35. b | 36. a | 37. b | 38. b | 39. a | 40. b |
| 41. a | | | | | | | | | |

## Chapter 4

| | | | | | | | | | |
|---|---|---|---|---|---|---|---|---|---|
| 1. a | 2. b | 3. a | 4. b | 5. b | 6. a | 7. a | 8. a | 9. a | 10. b |
| 11. a | 12. a | 13. b | 14. b | 15. a | 16. a | 17. a | 18. a | 19. a | 20. b |
| 21. a | 22. b | 23. b | 24. b | 25. a | 26. a | 27. a | 28. a | 29. b | 30. b |
| 31. a | 32. b | 33. b | 34. b | 35. b | 36. a | 37. a | 38. b | 39. b | 40. b |
| 41. b | 42. b | 43. b | | | | | | | |

## Chapter 5

| | | | | | | | | | |
|---|---|---|---|---|---|---|---|---|---|
| 1. a | 2. b | 3. b | 4. a | 5. b | 6. b | 7. a | 8. a | 9. b | 10. a |
| 11. b | 12. b | 13. b | 14. b | 15. b | 16. b | 17. a | 18. b | 19. a | 20. a |
| 21. b | 22. a | 23. b | 24. b | 25. b | 26. a | 27. b | 28. b | 29. b | 30. b |
| 31. b | 32. a | 33. b | 34. a | 35. a | 36. b | | | | |

## Chapter 6

| | | | | | | | | | |
|---|---|---|---|---|---|---|---|---|---|
| 1. b | 2. b | 3. a | 4. b | 5. b | 6. a | 7. a | 8. b | 9. b | 10. a |
| 11. a | 12. a | 13. b | 14. a | 15. a | 16. a | 17. a | 18. b | 19. a | 20. a |
| 21. a | 22. b | 23. a | | | | | | | |

## Chapter 7

| | | | | | | | | | |
|---|---|---|---|---|---|---|---|---|---|
| 1. b | 2. a | 3. b | 4. a | 5. a | 6. a | 7. b | 8. a | 9. a | 10. b |
| 11. a | 12. b | 13. b | 14. a | 15. b | 16. b | 17. a | 18. b | 19. b | 20. a |
| 21. a | 22. b | 23. a | 24. b | 25. a | 26. a | 27. b | 28. b | | |

# ANSWER KEY

**Chapter 8**
| | | | | | | | | | |
|---|---|---|---|---|---|---|---|---|---|
| 1. a | 2. a | 3. b | 4. a | 5. b | 6. b | 7. b | 8. b | 9. b | 10. a |
| 11. a | 12. a | 13. b | 14. b | 15. a | 16. a | 17. a | 18. a | 19. a | 20. a |
| 21. a | 22. a | 23. a | 24. a | 25. b | 26. b | 27. b | 28. b | 29. a | 30. b |
| 31. a | 32. b | 33. a | 34. a | 35. a | 36. b | | | | |

**Chapter 9**
| | | | | | | | | | |
|---|---|---|---|---|---|---|---|---|---|
| 1. a | 2. a | 3. b | 4. b | 5. b | 6. a | 7. b | 8. b | 9. a | 10. a |
| 11. a | 12. b | 13. b | 14. a | 15. a | 16. b | 17. b | 18. a | 19. b | 20. a |
| 21. a | 22. b | 23. b | 24. b | | | | | | |

**Chapter 10**
| | | | | | | | | | |
|---|---|---|---|---|---|---|---|---|---|
| 1. b | 2. a | 3. a | 4. b | 5. b | 6. a | 7. b | 8. b | 9. a | 10. b |
| 11. b | 12. b | 13. a | 14. a | 15. b | 16. a | 17. b | 18. a | 19. b | 20. b |
| 21. a | 22. b | 23. a | 24. a | 25. b | 26. a | 27. a | 28. a | | |

**Chapter 11**
| | | | | | | | | | |
|---|---|---|---|---|---|---|---|---|---|
| 1. b | 2. b | 3. a | 4. a | 5. b | 6. a | 7. b | 8. a | 9. a | 10. a |
| 11. a | 12. b | 13. b | 14. a | 15. b | 16. a | 17. a | 18. a | 19. b | 20. b |
| 21. b | 22. a | 23. a | 24. a | 25. b | 26. b | 27. b | 28. b | 29. a | 30. b |

**Chapter 12**
| | | | | | | | | | |
|---|---|---|---|---|---|---|---|---|---|
| 1. a | 2. b | 3. b | 4. b | 5. b | 6. b | 7. a | 8. a | 9. b | 10. b |
| 11. a | 12. a | 13. b | 14. b | 15. b | 16. b | 17. a | 18. a | 19. b | 20. b |
| 21. b | 22. b | 23. b | 24. a | 25. b | 26. a | 27. a | 28. a | 29. a | |

**Chapter 13**
| | | | | | | | | | |
|---|---|---|---|---|---|---|---|---|---|
| 1. b | 2. a | 3. a | 4. b | 5. a | 6. b | 7. a | 8. a | 9. b | 10. b |
| 11. b | 12. b | 13. b | 14. b | 15. a | 16. a | 17. a | 18. b | 19. b | 20. a |

**Chapter 14**
| | | | | | | | | | |
|---|---|---|---|---|---|---|---|---|---|
| 1. a | 2. a | 3. b | 4. a | 5. a | 6. b | 7. b | 8. b | 9. a | 10. b |
| 11. b | 12. a | 13. a | 14. a | 15. a | 16. a | 17. a | 18. b | 19. a | 20. b |
| 21. a | 22. a | 23. a | 24. b | 25. a | 26. b | 27. b | 28. b | 29. b | 30. a |
| 31. b | 32. b | 33. b | 34. b | 35. b | 36. a | 37. b | 38. a | 39. b | |

**Chapter 15**
| | | | | | | | | | |
|---|---|---|---|---|---|---|---|---|---|
| 1. a | 2. b | 3. a | 4. a | 5. b | 6. b | 7. b | 8. b | 9. a | 10. a |
| 11. b | 12. a | 13. a | 14. a | 15. b | 16. a | 17. a | 18. b | 19. a | 20. b |
| 21. a | 22. b | 23. a | 24. a | 25. b | 26. a | 27. a | 28. b | 29. b | |

**Chapter 16**

1. b  2. a  3. a  4. a  5. b  6. a  7. b  8. a  9. b  10. a
11. a  12. a  13. b  14. a  15. a  16. b  17. b  18. b  19. b  20. a
21. b  22. b

**Chapter 17**

1. b  2. a  3. b  4. a  5. b  6. a  7. a  8. b  9. a  10. b
11. a  12. a  13. b  14. a  15. a  16. a  17. a  18. b  19. a  20. a
21. a  22. b

www.ingramcontent.com/pod-product-compliance
Lightning Source LLC
Chambersburg PA
CBHW082051230426
43670CB00016B/2850